THE RESCUE OF SCIENCE AND LEARNING

The Authors

STEPHEN DUGGAN, Ph.D., LL.D., Litt.D., L.H.D.

Director Emeritus of the Institute of International Education. Formerly Professor of Political Science at the College of the City of New York.

BETTY DRURY, A.B., A.M.

Formerly Research Associate, Committee for the Study of Recent Immigration from Europe, Administrative Assistant, American Christian Committee for Refugees. Secretary for Personnel, Church World Service.

The Rescue of
Science and Learning

*The Story of the Emergency Committee
In Aid of Displaced Foreign Scholars*

By STEPHEN DUGGAN

Pierce Hayden

CHAIRMAN OF THE EMERGENCY COMMITTEE

and BETTY DRURY

EXECUTIVE SECRETARY TO THE EMERGENCY
COMMITTEE

THE MACMILLAN COMPANY · NEW YORK

THE EMERGENCY COMMITTEE IN AID OF DISPLACED FOREIGN SCHOLARS

EXECUTIVE COMMITTEE
Stephen Duggan, *Chairman*

Nelson P. Mead, *Secretary*
Fred M. Stein, *Treasurer*
Alfred E. Cohn, *Assistant Treasurer*
Frank Aydelotte
L. C. Dunn
*† Livingston Farrand

*Bernard Flexner
Alvin Johnson
Hertha Kraus
Charles J. Liebman
Henry Allen Moe
Charles A. Riegelman
Harlow Shapley

Betty Drury, *Executive Secretary*

GENERAL COMMITTEE
*Thomas S. Baker, *Carnegie Institute of Technology*
*Lotus D. Coffman, *University of Minnesota*
*Sir Arthur Currie, *McGill University*
Harold Willis Dodds, *Princeton University*
Sidney B. Fay, *Harvard University*
Abraham Flexner, *Institute for Advanced Study*
*Harry A. Garfield, *Williams College*
Robert M. Hutchins, *University of Chicago*
*James H. Kirkland, *Vanderbilt University*
Henry N. MacCracken, *Vassar College*
Robert A. Millikan, *California Institute of Technology*
Wesley C. Mitchell, *Columbia University*
Harold G. Moulton, *Brookings Institution*
*William A. Neilson, *Smith College*
*George Norlin, *University of Colorado*
Marion Edwards Park, *Bryn Mawr College*
Walter Dill Scott, *Northwestern University*
Robert G. Sproul, *University of California*
Oswald Veblen, *Institute for Advanced Study*
Ray Lyman Wilbur, *Stanford University*
Ernest H. Wilkins, *Oberlin College*
*Mary E. Woolley, *Mount Holyoke College*

---

* Now deceased.
† Chairman, 1933–1939.

Foreword

T HE authors of this little book finish a labor of love with which they have been associated for fourteen years, a labor suggested by the title of the book. During that long period, like all the members of the Emergency Committee, they have learned to admire the fortitude of the splendid scholars uprooted from their homes and driven from their universities, to seek a refuge anywhere in which to start life anew, usually in a place of strange language and customs. Though the task has not been fully completed, the pressing emergency ended with the success of the United Nations in the war.

The authors met with many difficulties: the loss by the scholars of credentials and other documents in the haste of their exit from Germany and the overrun countries; the unwillingness of scholars to bare their lives lest they appear as applicants for charity; their hesitancy to tell all the facts about their circumstances because of fear of reprisals to loved ones at home; reluctance to describe candidly their experiences in their college environment here lest they be considered guilty of ingratitude. The report owes much to the assistance of college administrators who provided critical information in Chapter X that might not have been otherwise obtainable. The reader will find unusually important, Chapter IX, "The Displaced Scholars Speak for Themselves."

Attention must also be directed to the informative Appendices, where material covered in the body of the book is presented in statistical and tabular form. To the college and university administrators the authors extend their thanks as they do to the foundations and organizations which so generously supported the program of the Emergency Committee and so freely supplied information. To the Executive Committee the authors wish to record their gratitude for the confidence so continuously extended to them. They take pleasure in acknowledging their indebtedness to Philip R. V. Curoe, Professor of Education at Hunter College, who read the entire manuscript and made excellent suggestions concerning structure, and to Miss Agnes Dowd and Mrs. William Stovall of the Institute of International Education who typed the manuscript.

The book has an unusual innovation: the story of the origin and organization of the Emergency Committee forms not the first but the last chapter. The hero of the book is the Displaced Scholar with his experiences during his exile and search for a place where he might again teach and pursue his researches. The authors did not want that stirring story diminished in its interest by starting the book with a description of the mechanics of the organization of the Emergency Committee. That is an absorbing story in itself, and no reader will want to miss learning of the indebtedness of the Emergency Committee to the university scholars and administrators who rallied with enthusiasm to the relief of the Displaced Foreign Scholars as described in Chapter XI.

The authors have tried to make this story of the displaced scholars as complete as possible without undue repetition of details, though some slight reiteration has been inevitable. There has been a division of labor: most of the text including interpretation and arrangement has been supplied by Dr.

Duggan, much of the illustrative material by Miss Drury. But dealing with hundreds of persons, many of whom have moved from one institution to another before becoming finally established, has presented obstacles to completeness. The epic of the displaced scholar cannot be written until his experiences in other lands become available. This little book is a contribution toward an understanding of the experiences he encountered in the United States. It is submitted to the public in the hope that, despite its inadequacies, it will serve as a record of an inspiring achievement.

STEPHEN DUGGAN
BETTY DRURY

Contents

xi

APPENDIX

THE RESCUE OF SCIENCE AND LEARNING

CHAPTER I

The Exodus of Scholars from Germany

IN 1453 Constantinople fell to the Turks and the Byzantine empire ceased to exist. The Turks were rude warriors to whom learning and schools meant very little, and they were regarded by the Greeks as barbarians—which at that time they were. Even before 1453 some scholars foreseeing the fall of the city had fled to Italy and the West, but that year every scholar who could escape did so. They received an enthusiastic welcome, for what was afterwards known as the Renaissance had already begun. Petrarch (1304–1374), "the first modern man," was the very embodiment of the spirit of the early Renaissance—that Latin movement which turned attention from the medieval study of patristic literature to the great literary figures of the Roman period. But Petrarch and his associates knew little or no Greek, and it was not until the Byzantine scholars arrived in Italy and started schools for the teaching of the Greek language and literature that a wave of enthusiasm for the Greek view of life gradually spread throughout the West.

The Renaissance was what its name signifies: a rebirth, a rebirth of a long-forgotten way of looking at life, the pre-Christian way. Joy of living, interest in the beauties and wonders of nature, the wish to know more of man's social relations, of his real desires, ambitions, and duties grew with every year. "Otherworldliness" began to give way to the

1

human interests of this world. Hence the leaders of the movement were called *humanists;* the movement itself, *humanism;*
and the content of their studies and teaching, the *humanities,*
as against the "divinities" of the medieval period. The study
of human affairs was to be found not in the works of the
Fathers of the Church but in the literature of Greece and
Rome. That is what is meant by the Revival of Learning to
which the displaced Greek scholars made so large a contribution. It was a great progressive movement in the history of
humanity.

Almost five hundred years later, in 1933, another barbarism
far worse than the Turkish afflicted humanity—Nazism. The
Turk was frank and forthright. He offered alternatives to
the conquered: the sword, conversion, or tribute. There was
no frankness about Nazism. It was founded upon the basest
form of deceit. It professed to offer the people of Germany
where it arose—torn at the time by internecine strife—a
stabilized life, a better standard of living, a greater degree of
security. As a matter of fact the leaders of the Nazi movement
determined from the very beginning to use any means to
realize their end: the re-forming of the German nation to
become the instrument of world dominance through force.
Lying, breaking of promises and ignoring of commitments,
violation of treaties and invasion of neighboring countries
without warning—these measures were unhesitatingly
adopted. For opponents of the new regime the alternatives
were not the sword but the horrors of the concentration camp,
not tribute but the looting of their property. As to conversion,
alas, millions, possibly the majority of the German citizenry,
accepted the new doctrine!

The Nazi objective internally was to make the government
totalitarian; that is, to vest in it total control of the life and
fortune of every individual German. The State was to be

everything, the individual to count for nothing. What an individual was allowed to say, orally or in print, and how he was to act was determined by the government. There was no redress, for the courts were muzzled, like the press and the platform. Any person opposing the government was to be suppressed by imprisonment, internment in a concentration camp, or death. Those arrested, if they were not put to death, were treated with the greatest cruelty and brutality.

To accomplish their aim the Nazis isolated the German people from the influence of the rest of the world by control of the instruments of mass education: the press, the radio, and the cinema. Propaganda within Germany by means of those instruments became intense; but to obtain control of the minds of men it was necessary to control the schools and the universities. There was not great difficulty with the schools, but the universities presented a different problem. In them existed the tradition of *Lern- und Lehrfreiheit,* to which many professors were devotedly loyal. The Nazis were determined to get rid of all such and replace them with professors who would teach the doctrines of "blood and soil," and "racism"—that is, the inferiority to the Germans of all other races, especially Slavs and Jews. Only in that way could the Nazis achieve the New Order "that was to last a thousand years." *Lern- und Lehrfreiheit* disappeared at once. Only such views of history, sociology, philosophy, and scholarship generally might be taught as were held to be in conformity to Nazi principles. All teachers were to be *gleichgeschaltet*— that is, coordinated, made to conform. In short the school and the university became propaganda machines to indoctrinate their students with the Nazi philosophy of race, religion, international relations, and life generally. As Hartshorne puts it in his admirable book, "The university had . . . lost the last vestige of independence which could have distinguished it from a pure State institution—and lost it at the expense of the students." [1] In order to maintain within Germany a *cordon sanitaire* to prevent the reception of opposing views, books with suspected contents were burnt, and listening to foreign radio broadcasts and reading of foreign newspapers were forbidden on pain of imprisonment. Persons suspected of holding radical views, communistic, socialistic, or liberal, were arrested. They seldom received a trial and usually suffered confiscation of property. Professors holding liberal and tolerant views were driven from the university. They were not merely debarred from teaching and research; they were not allowed to make a living at all. Because Hitler had decided from the beginning of his regime to destroy the Jewish people as far as he could, the hounding of Jewish scholars from their chairs in the universities was undertaken with particular vigor. Their flight became a veritable exodus. Fanaticism has never counted the cost of its actions. The Nazis forged ahead with their activities regardless of consequences, finally bringing intellectual sterility to the cultural life of Germany and almost utter destruction to its political and economic life.

THE FLIGHT OF THE SCHOLARS

As in the case of the Greek scholars of Byzantium some of the German scholars anticipated what might happen and fled from Germany—usually deprived of most of their possessions through various underhand devices of the Nazis. As the power of the Nazis grew, and as opposition declined, barefaced stealing accompanied by inhuman brutality became the order of the day. The Greek scholars who fled from the Turks had

---

[1] Edward Yarnall Hartshorne, Jr., *The German Universities and National Socialism* (Cambridge: Harvard University Press, 1937), p. 47.

received an enthusiastic welcome in the countries of the West, usually lands of admittedly inferior culture. This was not always true of the German scholars. The countries of Western and Northern Europe to which they first fled boasted of as high civilization and culture as Germany, and the scholars' placement would be a matter of their fitting in where they could, in the universities of those countries. Moreover, while they could contribute a great deal to scholarship because of their eminence in their fields of learning, they could not be expected to become part cause of such a revolution in culture as was true of the displaced Greek scholars during the Renaissance.

The democratic neighbors of Germany received the refugee scholars with great sympathy and offered them vital assistance. Many displaced scholars were absorbed in the schools and universities as teachers and research experts. Others found places in financial and industrial corporations. The Academic Assistance Council of England (later to become the Society for the Protection of Science and Learning) was formed to give immediate succor to the refugee scholars and to investigate every possibility of placement. No praise can be too high to give to this distinguished body of British scholars and men of affairs for their unceasing efforts in behalf of the displaced German professors. The French committee, Association Universelle pour les Exilés Allemands, also did yeoman service in securing positions for them in universities and lycées and, as writers, on newspapers and magazines. Much assistance was given also by the smaller neighbors of Germany: Holland, Belgium, Switzerland, and the Scandinavian countries. The scholars gladly settled down with their families at a reduced standard of living and took up once more their researches and teaching. Alas, in a very few years when the Nazi armies overran almost all Europe, there was nothing for the exiled scholars to do but flee from their new homes and seek refuge overseas in the Western Hemisphere.

It was natural that the friends of freedom and of scholarship should look hopefully across the Atlantic to the rich United States with its hundreds of colleges and universities for places that might be found for distinguished teachers and research scholars. It was reasonable to believe that in all probability more opportunities of this kind existed in the United States than in all the rest of the world combined. The first step toward taking advantage of those opportunities was to secure an agency which would serve as intermediary. Such an agency was found in the Institute of International Education, which had been established close after the First World War as an instrument to develop understanding and good will between the people of the United States and the peoples of other countries, by means of educational exchanges. That the Institute was peculiarly well fitted to undertake this work was evident. Among its manifold achievements it had helped to organize the Russian Student Fund for refugees from the Bolshevik Revolution of 1917. The Fund succeeded by 1933 in securing places on scholarships for more than six hundred Russian students in American institutions of higher education and for a few English-speaking Russian professors as teachers. It was knowledge of the *raison d'être* of the Institute and of its accomplishment in the field that brought about the visit to the Institute in the early days of May, 1933, of Dr. Alfred E. Cohn, a distinguished scientist of the Rockefeller Institute for Medical Research, Bernard Flexner, an eminent lawyer and philanthropist, and Fred M. Stein, a leader in philanthropies in New York City. Their concern was to discuss with the Director of the Institute, Dr. Stephen Duggan, a method whereby assistance might be extended to the scholars who had fled to the United States. The celebrated New York philanthropist Felix M. Warburg had already discussed with these gentlemen the urgent necessity of stimulating action in the United States to assist the refugee scholars, and Dr. Alan Gregg, Director of Medical Sciences of the Rockefeller Foundation, had suggested the Institute of International Education as the place where advice might well be secured that would serve their purpose. An organizing committee consisting of Dr. Cohn, Mr. Flexner, Mr. Stein, and Dr. Duggan was formed, with the name Emergency Committee in Aid of Displaced German Scholars.[2] The Committee which developed from the planning of these men and from their consultation with educators throughout the United States functioned for twelve years as an agency which raised funds in behalf of displaced scholars and made these funds available primarily through a program of grants-in-aid to colleges, universities and learned institutions, and later through a special fellowship project which served artists, writers and other professional people as well. The Committee gave no direct relief. Foundations provided the major part of its funds, which were augmented from time to time by generous gifts from a number of individual contributors.

---

[2] On November 9, 1938, the Committee's name was changed to Emergency Committee in Aid of Displaced Foreign Scholars—to include refugee professors from all countries of Western Europe overrun by the Nazi armies. The origin, organization, and policies of the Emergency Committee in Aid of Displaced Foreign Scholars are fully described in Chapter XI.

CHAPTER II

The Displaced Scholar Before the Exodus

MUCH information concerning the plight of the displaced scholars was secured by correspondence even before they left Germany. This was particularly true of the early arrivals and of the most distinguished among the displaced scholars, whether they later secured positions under the auspices of this committee or under circumstances of which the Committee was informed. The letter which follows illustrates the kind of treatment the displaced scholar received in the early days of the Nazi regime. It portrays the meanness of the treatment meted out—treatment, however, which had not yet sunk to the level of absolute brutality. It also illustrates the deteriorating influence of the persecutions upon the morality of associates of displaced scholars in the German universities. The statements which follow this letter describe the terror under which the displaced scholars lived a few years later:*

Confidential   3rd August, 1934
Dear Sir:
  I thank you very much for the kind interest you take in my fate. Your question is not easily answered in one sentence, because the Government took great care to veil the reasons for my dismissal: that there was a *Misstimmung* against me among the

---

* These letters are not translations, but were written in English by German-speaking scholars.

8

"students." In fact, a memorandum against me had been drawn up to the effect

1. That my wife was non-Aryan—her mother comes from absolutely Aryan family, her father was a Protestant, but her grandfather was a Jew; and
2. That I posed as a friend of the new movement and was not so in my heart.

It was construed into a "severe attack on National Socialism" that I had suggested as a subject for an optional examination paper to discuss "How far may Carlyle be considered a precursor of National Socialism?" This memorandum was not drawn up by the "students," but by my former assistant, Dr.   , because it contains dicta of mine and criticism of the movement which I had made only privately to Dr.   , who owes very much to me, but got impatient because at the age of 41 years he had not been offered a professorship, and got it into his head that that was my fault. In order to avoid the impression that this was an act of private revenge, Dr.   secured the assistance of a young student who was the official "leader" of the new philological students. These men were staunch adherents of the Nazi movement. Everybody who knows anything about university life here will be able to testify to the fact that I was one of the most popular professors; I had been chosen Honorary President by two students' clubs, and had been made an Honorary Member of two others.

My present position is that of an Emeritus Professor. Officially I have all the rights of an Emeritus but, de facto, I am debarred from exercising most of them: I am not allowed to lecture any more, to hold examinations, to perform any public functions, etc. When I was elected a Corresponding Fellow of the British Academy, the papers did not dare to bring a notice about it. You can imagine that, under such circumstances, I feel an outlaw here and would gladly leave the place. Being a passionate teacher and lecturer, however, I should like very much, temporarily, to exercise such functions. If you could help me to find such opportunities, I should be most grateful to you.

Thanking you once more most heartily for your very kind exertions on my behalf, I remain

Yours very truly,

A legal scholar has provided this thoughtful comment which dates from November, 1939 (the italics are our own):

At the beginning of the Hitler revolution there were a good deal of illegal brutalities exercised by the stormtroopers and by private persons. These facts are well known in the United States, and most of these "atrocity stories" really happened. After a few weeks, however, these irregularities ceased more and more. The fact that the most prominent German émigrés left Germany in the first phase of the Hitler revolution caused the impression abroad that the situation of the spring of 1933 still prevailed. This was not true.

Since the summer of 1933, terror is in the hands of the authorities; the *"legal illegality"* . . . *is far more dangerous than the brutalities of the first period.* Nobody has any chance to hide from these attacks. The bureaucratic machine works with an efficiency which never can be attained by masses which do not control an apparatus. When Hitler came to power he controlled a bureaucracy which is perhaps the most efficient in the world. The activities of unorganized groups which could not but disturb the systematic work of the organs of the Prerogative State were therefore forbidden. The formal legitimacy of the Nazi revolution—as far as it exists—is a means of oppression . . .

The process of Nazification which was spread out in Germany over many years took in Austria only a few weeks. In Austria radical Nazis were substituted for the old bureaucracy whereas in Germany the old bureaucracy was almost wholly taken over.

A letter from Europe describing the arrest of Nobel Prize winners in Austria after its occupation by the Nazis is indicative of the increasing brutality of the Nazi government:

The third Nobel Prize man of   University, Professor   , has been forced by threats to his life to sign a humiliating declaration that he recognizes that he has been wrong in his views of the Nazi regime and now realizes with deep shame the real greatness of the Führer.

Hamilton Basso, in an article on the distinguished philosopher, Jean Wahl, which appeared in *The New Yorker* May

12, 1945, describes certain aspects of the Nazi occupation of Paris as they affected university teachers:

> On the morning of June 13, 1940, when the first advance units of the German Army were entering Paris, Wahl was caught in the disintegration of the life of a great city. It seemed wise for him to leave Paris, since he is a Jew and the Nazis could not be expected to be more tolerant of French Jews than of German Jews . . .
>
> Two months later, after the crumbling of the Third Republic, the setting up of Vichy, and the division of France into two zones . . . Wahl received word that the Sorbonne was planning to go on as usual and that his old post was waiting for him. . . . The Sorbonne opened quietly for the fall term and he began holding his classes again . . . The Germans were now in their "correct," or ingratiating, period, when they made a cult of surface politeness while beginning the reign of terror in France that is only now being fully exposed. On Armistice Day, November 11, 1940, there was a demonstration of Sorbonne students in the Place de la Concorde. The principal sentiment expressed was "Death to the Germans!" In reprisal, the Sorbonne was closed for a time. When it reopened, Wahl was no longer a member of the faculty. The Germans had decided that the time had come for all Jewish teachers in France to be dismissed from their posts.
>
> . . . The atmosphere of "correctness" was beginning to give way to the chill of terror. The Gestapo had set up its headquarters on the Avenue Foch, in a splendid mansion it had appropriated, and in Paris there were now the same hushed whispers that had been woven into the fabric of occupation from Norway to Czechoslovakia. . . .

Wahl had the rare experience during the occupation of France of being released from internment following receipt of an invitation to join the faculty of a foreign institution. Liberation came after a series of less happy circumstances— after his dismissal by the Germans from his French university post, questioning by the Gestapo, and imprisonment.

Wahl was held in La Santé [prison] for thirty-six days; then, in August, 1941, he was sent to the concentration camp the Germans had set up at Drancy, just outside Paris. It consisted of twenty barracks, housing thirty-five hundred men. They were all Jews, and the Germans treated them with characteristic harshness. "In that respect," Wahl recalls, "it was worse than the prison. There were people besides Jews in La Santé and the Germans take some care of people. They take no care whatsoever of Jews." . . .

Epidemic swept the camp, and as proper hospitalization was impossible, the Germans thought it best to release some of the prisoners.

His bad luck, though he didn't know it, was about to end. The head doctor at Drancy was a Frenchman. The list of prisoners to be released had to be approved by him. He had been told, by the head nurse, of Wahl's appointment to the faculty of the New School. He didn't know anything about the New School, but his respect for learning was enough to make him, unknown to the Germans, add Wahl's name to the list at the last minute. The next morning Wahl walked through the gates of Drancy. He had been in the camp sixty-four days.

For many years before the events described took place in the occupied countries, terrorism had been driving university teachers from their chairs in the German universities. The previous careers of these scholars were of the same pattern. Just as in the United States a college teacher usually passed through the grades of instructor, assistant professor, and associate professor before becoming a professor of full grade, so in Germany a university teacher was always a Privatdozent before becoming a professor and might have held the position of Dozent at first.[1] Until the founding of

---

[1] "In contradistinction to this formalized status [that of Privatdozent], the Dozent held a much less formal position, for which the 'Visiting Lecturer' is perhaps the best analogy. This does not, however, imply a purely temporary position. Quite a number of Dozenten in technical and commercial colleges

the Republic a Privatdozent could offer a course at a university but received no official salary, his compensation being the fee paid by the students taking his course. It is a common practice in the United States to call a teacher of lower grade in one institution to a professorship in another. The same practice holds true in Germany.

The existence of the émigré professors, Privatdozenten, and other academicians previous to the exodus may be illustrated by the career of the late historian, Arthur Rosenberg. A Privatdozent at the University of Berlin from 1914 to 1930 (and part of that time a member of the German Reichstag), he became a professor at his university in 1930 and held that rank until 1933, when his exile began. Other displaced German scholars—and there were unhappily a considerable number—have known exile several times, as did Professor E. S. Gumbel who, a refugee from the University of Heidelberg, became a faculty member of the University of Lyon before his flight to the United States after the Nazi occupation of France. His experience was similar to, though not as unhappy as, that of the late Alexander Pekelis of whom Dr. Alvin Johnson has written:

Launched into the world in 1902, in what was then the peaceful city of Odessa, Pekelis exhibited from his early youth an unconquerable ambition for scholarly achievement. The rise of bolshevism and the wrecking of the Russian universities drove him out of Russia in 1920, to study in the Universities of Leipzig and Vienna. Having been deprived of his Russian citizenship in 1922, he became a man without a country, a situation very unfavorable to advancement in the German university world.

He traveled to Italy on a Nansen passport, studied law at the University of Florence, where he won his doctorate with distinc-

---

served for an indefinite period under this title. As a general rule, the Dozent confined his activity less exclusively to university teaching, and was usually a man who, for reasons of expert knowledge in a special field, was asked to join the teaching staff."—Professor Adolph Lowe, Institute of World Affairs, New School for Social Research.

tion; became an Italian citizen and set out on what promised to be a brilliant career as professor of law. The rise of fascism drove him from his chair at the University of Rome and compelled him to emigrate to America, where he joined the graduate faculty of the New School for Social Research in 1941.[2]

The reasons which drove these scholars from Germany varied. They usually stemmed from race and religion. For example, one academician had to flee because he was the grandson of a niece of Felix Mendelssohn and hence a "non-Aryan." Another—and there were many such—was displaced because his wife's grandmother was Jewish.

There were many others, however, who left not because of race or religion but because of outraged principles. One scholar and his wife who were "pure Aryan" left solely because he refused to subscribe to Nazi racial beliefs. A celebrated mathematician, said to be one of the few in the world capable of keeping pace with Einstein, abandoned his university post as a protest against the removal of Jewish faculty members. One prominent philosopher voluntarily gave up his brilliant career at the Prussian Academy of Sciences in Berlin as a demonstration against the practice of the German authorities in removing professors for any reasons other than scholastic ones. Another widely respected professor of philosophy was "ousted from his chair in the University of Rostock because of his manly stand in demanding, before taking an oath to support the policies of the present German government, a clear guarantee that the commitment of the oath would leave unimpaired his freedom to seek and teach the truth."

There were still other reasons for the ousting of professors. One distinguished economist was driven from his university

---

[2] "Tribute to Dr. Pekelis," by Alvin Johnson, *New York Times,* Jan. 1, 1947.

post in 1933 "at the request of the National Socialist student organization." An eminent woman professor had to leave her institution, not because of her race or religion but because she was a woman and the Nazis were opposed to women in institutions of higher education. So it went down the line with the pattern repeated in each country as it was overrun by the Nazis.

The lot of displaced Jewish professors within the Nazi-dominated countries was indeed harsh. University employment was forbidden, and libraries and research facilities were closed to them. The enjoyment of public parks was often denied, and they were inevitably saddened by the hostility which greeted their children. As in Germany they had to wear the yellow Star of David on their sleeves.[3] Some were fortunate enough to emigrate at once. Many of those fled to England; others as already stated were able to get to the New World. Still others, however, sought to leave Europe but had neither the means which would have made the journey possible nor entrée to a country where a post could be secured. A number chose to remain in their homeland, devoting themselves to a cloistered life of study and research among their own books and papers. It was the fate of some of these to wait many years for liberation.

Many were incarcerated. One world-renowned medical scientist was taken into "protective custody" by the Nazis. While there his youngest son was beaten in prison because pressure was brought from outside to release the father. The record of another scholar states: "He was removed from his Directorship. . . . He was not allowed to use the library or museum, even though many of the most significant objects in

---

[3] It was to the eternal credit of King Christian IX of Denmark that, when the German Occupation threatened to compel Danish Jews to wear the Star of David, he told the Germans that he would be the first to do so. The Germans dropped the demand.

the museum had been procured by him. Finally, all his property was confiscated, and he was obliged to borrow three
thousand dollars from his friends to get out of Germany.
The appointment which he received [in the United States]
was the only thing that saved him from death in a concentration camp." Professor Haber, famous for his synthesis of
ammonia, fled to Switzerland and died there a suicide.

Some of these fine scholars left beleaguered cities on foot,
fleeing with hordes of civilians over roads which were torn
by bombing and strafing raids, to take refuge with other
refugees in cellars and ruined churches. Some found temporary though precarious asylum in cities of transit, waiting
for the help of foreign rescue committees. Varian Fry of the
Emergency Rescue Committee, to whose help so many distinguished refugees owed their lives, tells of one among
many such cases:

> Professor Dietrich von Hildebrand, formerly of the University
> of Vienna, was hiding with his wife in an apartment on the corner
> of the rue Breteuil and the rue Grignan. As one of the most
> prominent of the Austrian [anti-Nazi] refugees, Professor von
> Hildebrand was in danger of extradition under Article 19, Swiss
> passport or no Swiss passport, and I had agreed to help him
> escape.[4]

Some crossed the Pyrenees on foot to escape from France
after the German occupation; others were smuggled across
borders by car and motor lorry. Of one scholar of international law the report states: "When the Germans invaded
Poland, he escaped; was wounded by the Germans, hid for
several months in the forests of Poland, and then finally
was able to reach nearby Lithuania." These personal his-
tories might be multiplied indefinitely.

---

[4] Varian Fry, *Surrender on Demand* (New York: Random House, 1945),
p. 27.

PLACEMENT OF THE SCHOLARS IN THE UNITED STATES

Once in the United States, the fate of these men and women varied. Some received calls at once to distinguished universities; other, less fortunate although often no less important in their fields of work, lived in obscurity for many years. Some were fortunate to have the help of interested organizations—the Rockefeller Foundation, the Oberlaender Trust, the service agencies, or our own organization. To others the years of waiting were years of hardship. Some tutored, or labored at small salaries in impoverished schools and academies without the wherewithal to buy adequate clothing, pay for much-needed medical and dental care, or send help overseas to even more destitute relatives. In fact it was not easy for the foreigner, intellectual or nonintellectual, to comprehend the nature and extent of the difficulties he had to face in the new country. Times were unexpectedly bad in 1933 and the years immediately succeeding. The United States, long considered a land of promise, was only beginning to work its way out of the depression. Jobs of any kind were hard to find. The immigrant, greeted with good humor and a sympathetic manner by American friends and colleagues in his efforts to find work, was often misled into taking this interest as a promise of a job. John Whyte has written of this misunderstanding out of the wealth of his experience with German scholars:

Germans frequently mistake a friendly reception of themselves and their projects for genuine interest and hence meet with cruel disappointments. A German looking for a position or for help of some kind may be met with, "I'll see what I can do for you," or "I'll consider you for the position," which, if nothing more definite is added, such as "Call me up again in a few days," or "I'll let you know by next Monday," is likely to be merely an evidence of friendliness or sympathy. In North Germany, where people are much more forthright, such friendliness might be considered as very encouraging to the candidate or to his project.[5]

Saddest of all, perhaps, but typical of a few, was the plight of the celebrated scholar who came to the New World expecting the same warm welcome and requests for scholarly collaboration as had invariably greeted him in happier days:

As a scientist he was known in many lands and everywhere was received as a distinguished and honored guest. When the storm clouds of Naziism broke over Europe, we felt confident that somewhere among the many scientific institutions which so often had solicited his cooperation or which, even, had elected him their honorary member, there would be surely a place for him to continue his work in his chosen field. His years of experience, his standing as a scientist would undoubtedly be of value in trying to obtain employment in the United States.

And so he came to America.

But how different was it now. He who had been an esteemed collaborator, whose advice in special questions had always been appreciated, was, now, only an immigrant—one among the thousands of immigrants coming to America as a haven of refuge, seeking employment and a chance to begin life anew in a strange land. Not yet did he realize all this. Not until he had traveled throughout the country seeking out every scientific institution which might have need of his services and abilities. Bewildering and disheartening were the answers he received. Everyone was cordial but regretful. They would like to have him as a member of their staff, but their staff was complete, and unfortunately there were not sufficient funds to employ an additional member. [6]

This was, however, an unusual experience for a scholar of real distinction.

---

[5] John Whyte, *American Words and Ways* (New York: Viking Press, 1943), p. 142.

[6] From an address given before the Seventeenth Triennial Convention of the National Council of Jewish Women, Chicago, 1943.

Ultimately, no fewer than 459 of the 613 university personnel known to the Emergency Committee through its own files (plus 70-odd academicians from an additional group of 94 of whom it learned from the Committee for the Study of Recent Immigration from Europe) found opportunity to teach or carry on research in American colleges or universities. Access to their own particular field or profession was thus by no means closed to the refugee scholars in this country; on the contrary many of them became firmly established in institutions of higher learning, and attained positions of eminence.

However, not all European academicians could follow academic careers. One former professor of medicine obtained an appointment on the staff of the chief medical examiner of a large eastern city; another appeared as a member of a medical advisory board in connection with Selective Service. Laboratory work on heart, hormones, and vitamin testing claimed quite a number. It was to be expected that university scientists who had contrived formulas for the manufacturing of adhesives for the leather industry, for the production of artificial meat flavors, for cosmetic preparations, for metal polishes, or who had labored to give soap powders special virtue, might, when necessary, by-pass the university for business and industry. Refugee academicians secured places in the Eastman Kodak Company, the Shell Development Company, the General Electric Company, the United States Radium Corporation, the United States Steel Corporation, the California Conference of Real Estate Taxpayers. Others found posts in public health departments, at the Rockefeller Institute for Medical Research, at the Federal Security Agency, in the Office of Price Administration, at the Saratoga Springs Authority, in the Fish and Wildlife Service of the Department of the Interior.

Like the professorial and university group, nonuniversity teachers, scholars, and scientists suffered greatly as a result of Nazi oppression. Although the Emergency Committee's primary concern was not with this group, a great deal of material concerning it came to the Committee's files. For teachers and many engaged in research, as for the university professors, conditions in Europe became unbearable. Race and creed forced many of them to leave. Others gave up their professional chances rather than capitulate to a government of which they could not in conscience approve. The concentration camps yawned for some, and the names of Dachau and Gurs appear constantly in the records. Not at all uncommon was the history of the former Gymnasium teacher who, having declined to become a Russian citizen during his residence in the Soviet Union, was expelled from that country in January, 1936, only to be sent by the Germans in the following July to the concentration camp of Esterwegen near the Dutch border, then to Sachsenhausen near Berlin, and lastly to Dachau.

To have suffered a period of imprisonment before exile is not the best preparation for life in a new country. Some diminution of personal attractiveness is bound to follow upon physical maltreatment. Lame bodies and scarred faces are a detriment when one goes job hunting. The man who has had his teeth knocked out by brutal prison guards is embarrassed to find himself mumbling when he asks for work. One record comments on a refugee applying for a teaching job:

This man has been deprived of whatever natural charm he may have possessed. He must have been very badly used in Germany for he gives every evidence of extreme nervousness and mental anguish. Some of his teeth are missing. His face is twisted as if by a partial stroke.

Many former teachers and research workers courageously took any work they could find. One woman did housework and acted as a governess. Another made artificial flowers; a third worked in a doll factory. A summer camp offered a place to a woman who taught needlework, crafts, and pattern making. A specialist in Romance languages gladly took a position with a banking firm as secretary and correspondent. The file of a Volkshochschule teacher stated, "She had nothing but a little light factory work from time to time when last contacted." An erstwhile teacher of mathematics and physics hired out as a domestic, became nursemaid to a six-year-old youngster, worked next in an accounting office, and—not concurrently—sewed uniforms in a factory. She later found her way back into teaching. Others became tutors, worked in settlement houses and summer camps, taught skiing, tennis, or horseback riding; and a few entered business and industry.

Similar were the experiences of the group of 329 men and women of scholarly or scientific attainments who had not, so far as the Committee knew, been formally affiliated with university life in Nazi, Fascist, or occupied countries or belonged at all to the teaching profession in Europe. There was a musicologist who carried on research for several years at a Western institution until his job folded up; answering an advertisement placed in the newspapers by a great industrial concern, he was employed as a day laborer at $6.00 a day. "When I met him," the field representative of the Emergency Committee wrote, "he had finished his first week of work there and was able to sit in his friend's home, smoke his pipe, admit his muscles were rather sore, and smile about it." A classical scholar succeeded at first only in finding employment as a dishwasher in a restaurant. "He handles garbage cans and freight elevators," stated his record, "meets many Greek, Italian, and Puerto Rican employees—but does not find them an aid to his Americanization. He has been able to save a little out of his $20 a week plus meals. His wife and parents, who could not escape from Europe, have probably been deported to Poland, or are dead."

The experience of the music historian was sobering, who worked as a machinist in a defense plant until his sensitive pianist's fingers were almost blunted. Another scholar who wrote to the Committee asking about his own prospects in the teaching field stated:

I moved to town last summer after the grant allowed to me by the Committee for last year had expired and have been here ever since doing research in my special field of legal history. I have not, however, been able yet to secure any position either as a teacher or as research worker and have been forced, after my savings ran out, to take work in a bakery.

As the Emergency Committee had found former university men and women outside their own grantees teaching in American institutions of higher learning, it was also interested to find that, among the 230 refugee nonuniversity teachers in the United States of whom it had partial records, at least twenty-eight secondary school teachers found appointments of varying degrees of permanency at American colleges and universities, particularly though by no means exclusively during the war years. In addition, a nursery school teacher and a physical education instructor found posts in American colleges, as did five representatives of teacher training and eight teachers of adult education. Eighteen other teachers of nonuniversity status found similar appointments, for the most part during the war years.

Evidence of the extent to which the Committee's own group finally became established, causing the Committee to feel that it could in justice draw its work to a close, was the fact that as time went on the problems which scholars and teachers brought for discussion to its office were less and less concerned with securing a bare livelihood or establishing professional status, and resembled more nearly the situations which faced American teachers already launched in the stream of academic life—need for higher salaries to meet the rising cost of living, desire to change jobs to obtain more favorable working conditions or better research facilities, and the necessity of keeping in touch with the changing labor market. The following excerpts from recorded interviews are typical of the trend which had become pronounced about 1943.

The situation of a woman teacher has wide applicability:

Came in to renew contact with us. Her mother died about a week ago. She is sad and disturbed. Should she remain at her small college, which is primarily vocational and does not recognize any need for art history, or should she break away and try to get back into the mainstream? She has no time for research, but finds the life there not unpleasant.

A distinguished economist voiced the reality which faced many older men:

Feels there is nothing for him here in academic life, since he is already sixty-three years old. Would like to go into government service.

The teaching career of a younger refugee scholar is interestingly illustrative of adjustment to American conditions:

Has been at State University for past year on leave of absence from ＿＿＿＿＿ College. Had rank of Associate Professor at $150 a month. Believed this experience was excellent for his Americanization. Will teach again this summer at the State University. Is under considerable financial pressure because of his large and growing family—parents, wife, one child, and another on the way. Can return to the ＿＿＿＿＿ College, but prefers not to. Learned a great deal from teaching Army Specialized Training Courses. States that he would not be interested in government employment, except perhaps in OSS. If he were called upon to work on Austrian problems, however, he would feel in duty bound to accept "as if drafted."

At the time the Emergency Committee closed its work in 1945, it had in its files by actual count, inclusive of its own grantees and fellows, partial records of 613 men and women who had lost their posts in European colleges, universities, or Hochschulen during the Hitler years, and who subsequently came to the United States. These records were sometimes quite full but were often incomplete. A letter of inquiry often came from a professor, while he was still in a foreign university town, seeking help in securing an academic post overseas and sometimes enclosing his curriculum vitae and list of publications. From such inadequate notes as the files offered, however, it was possible to piece together some related facts that contributed to a composite picture of the displaced academician as this Committee saw him.

Of the total group known to the Emergency Committee who had to give up hope of an academic career in Europe and who succeeded in reaching the United States, 582 were men and 31 were women. The largest number of these—166 —had been born between the years 1896 and 1905, so that they might have been anywhere from twenty-eight to thirty-seven when Hitler came into power. Of the entire group— which, it should be understood, included Emergency Committee academicians—some 366 had been professors, 74 had attained the rank of Privatdozent or its equivalent before being displaced, and 15 classified themselves as Dozenten.[7] The remainder fell into less readily identifiable groupings— "instructors," "researchers," "lecturers," and others, difficult

[7] See footnote 1, p. 12.

because of linguistic ambiguity to equate too surely to recognized university ranks. It should be borne in mind that, had more biographical material been available about certain others of the men and women in the Committee's files, this list of displaced university personnel later domiciled in the United States might have been increased.

The marital status of 387 of the group of 613 was known, and it appeared that 311 of this number were married, 65 single, 9 widowers or widows, and 2 divorced or separated.

The dates of arrival in the United States of 371 had been established as follows: 30 arrived in 1933; 32 in 1934; 15 in 1935; 20 in 1936; 15 in 1937; 43 in 1938; 97 in 1939; 59 in 1940; 50 in 1941; and 10 during 1942 and 1943 (none recorded during the last two years of the Committee's life). There is of course a reflection here of events in Europe— the outbreak of war, the fall of France, and the virtual cessation of emigration to this country while the United States was engaged in hostilities. Scanty information is available about visas: of 224 persons whose immigration status at the time of entry was known to the Committee, 210 entered on immigration visas.

The countries of birth, or of last known citizenship where the birthplace was not established, follow the pattern which might have been expected. Of the total number of 613 men and women in the academic group, data were available on 486, of whom more than half—248—came from Germany. The next largest group, 53, came from Austria. Poland and Italy each claimed 36, while France, Czechoslovakia, and Russia trailed with 26, 25, and 23 respectively. Hungary was represented by 13 academicians, Belgium by 8, Spain and Switzerland by 4 each, the Netherlands by 3, Estonia and Yugoslavia by 2 each, and Bulgaria, Denmark, and Norway by 1 each.

As already indicated, the files contained little to enlighten the curious as to the religious affiliations of the refugee scholars. The Emergency Committee never requested this information of the men and women who turned to it for assistance. Some chose to publish their allegiance to a particular faith, however, and about others newspaper clippings left no doubt. When every source has been considered, we are only able to say that, of 177 men and women whose affiliation was known to us, 82 were Jewish, 55 Protestants, 39 Roman Catholics, and 1 Eastern Orthodox.

No description of the group would be complete without a consideration of the disciplines they represented. Law was the favored field of interest, claiming 69 scholars out of the total group of 613, and 63 had devoted themselves to physics. Economics and chemistry followed with 54 and 53 adherents respectively. Language and literature, and medical sciences, came immediately after with 51 each. Other disciplines followed in this order: mathematics, 46; philosophy, 43; history, 41; art and archaeology, 32; psychology, 23; sociology, 19; biology, 14; music and musicology, 10; political science, 9; theology and religion, 7; engineering, 6; uncertain, 6; astronomy, 5; zoology, 4; anthropology, 3; education, 3; geology and geography, 1.

CHAPTER III

The Displaced Scholar in His New Environment

THE displaced scholars invited to our universities with the help of the Emergency Committee were in most cases men of distinction in European universities. There were several Nobel Prize holders among them. Fifteen were listed in *Who's Who in America* for 1944–1945 and thirty-eight in *American Men of Science* for 1944. The more fortunate were absorbed very soon into the faculties of our universities and scientific institutions. Others equally eminent were for years partially dependent upon the grants by the Emergency Committee to their institutions, for the country was slow in coming out of the depression. But financial difficulties confronting the displaced scholars constituted by no means the only obstacle in their adjustment to their new environment. The profound difference which existed between the administrative set-up of American and German institutions of higher education was a source of astonishment and sometimes of discomfort to the displaced foreign scholars. A professor in a German university is a man of research rather than a teacher. He delivers a few set lectures every week and otherwise has little contact with his students. The quiz and discussion as aids to the lecture system, which are such important and valuable aspects of the American system, are the exception

27

rather than the rule. They are restricted on the whole to the seminar, which consists of the small group of advanced students making a special and intensive study of some aspect of the professor's field. The small seminar group becomes intimately acquainted with the professor, but that is not true of the great majority of the students attending the professor's lectures.

Many former Gymnasium professors were placed in our colleges because the last two years of the German Gymnasium were the equivalent of the first two years of our college, if not of even higher rank. With rare exceptions the Gymnasium has no dormitories, the student living at home or in a pension if away from home. The Gymnasium is a place not merely of study but of grind. In it are found few of the extracurricular activities that form so large a part of college life in the United States. At the close of the day the Gymnasium student takes home a great deal of work for the next day; and it goes badly with him if he comes unprepared the following morning. The American student often does come unprepared —as President Wilson once said, "The side shows sometimes overshadowed the main tent." This was a strange situation to the German professor.

Moreover, the administration of an American university or college was very different from that of the German university or Gymnasium. The German professor who was invited to teach in a small American college learned to his amazement that it is not unusual for a professor to be assigned fifteen hours of teaching per week in addition to committee assignments. Furthermore, in our institutions of higher education a professor is appointed to serve upon numerous committees which consume much time in addition to his teaching duties. He assigns topics upon which the students write papers, which he must read and criticize. Not only in our colleges but in many of our universities, records are kept of students' attendance, whereas attendance in a German university is wholly voluntary. One of the fine characteristics of the American college is the friendly relationship that exists between the professor and the student, who is often invited to the professor's home. All these activities, which are an integral part of an American professor's life, use up a great deal of his time. The German professor is essentially a research scholar, however, and has had to adapt himself to these new and sometimes onerous conditions.

Some of the difficulties are well illustrated in the following extracts from a letter written by a fine displaced scholar who had received an invitation to teach in a small college in a midwestern state:

Our economics professor sent a telegram announcing his resignation exactly 72 hours before the classes were scheduled to start. The result was, that I was asked to take over most of his courses, bringing the number of courses offered by me to seven, and the number of lecture hours to 19 per week. You will understand that under such circumstances, which have not changed since, it is well nigh impossible to resume research work and writing. I write this with a good deal of regret, though not in the way of a complaint. I realize very well that this rather heavy load is a consequence of war conditions, and I take my extra load as part of war work.

He went on to touch upon another point sometimes mentioned in criticism of the refugee scholar—his alleged radicalism:

In my work I have, so far, not had any difficulties apart from a slight complaint concerning allegedly "radical" views in political economy. It was reported to me—in the way of a subtle "hint" —that unfortunately many colleges have had the experience that the refugee professor did not seem to have sympathy with the

American system of free enterprise, and that consequently most of them had transferred such professors from the Social Science Department of their respective schools to the Language Department.

. . . I am, and shall be, grateful to Dr. X and others for giving us refuge and for showing understanding and patience, but I am starting to look around for a more congenial place where I would, if possible, have some time for research, something that I am missing very much.

European scholars have commented frequently and some-times amusingly on the physical differences between American and European institutions of higher learning. Erna Barschak has contributed some diverting pages to the subject, from which the following excerpts are taken:

There were many more interesting and, to me, novel institutions which I was discovering. Drinking fountains everywhere—Americans seem to be especially fond of drinking water; pencil sharpeners fixed on the walls so that they cannot be misappropriated like their European counterparts which always disappear; a special mail service for the college population and—a supply office which provides pencils, ink and paper free of charge to the instructors! All this is just wonderful.

Were the colleges the products of the students, or were the students the products of the colleges? Her picture of the American student might have been drawn by the pen of any one of hundreds of European educators. Whether it will prove to be an accurate picture of postwar college youth is a question which time will answer:

My personal contact with the students was at first very much limited by the fact that I found it hard to distinguish among them. They looked so very much alike. I have found out by now that all American college students are eager to conform to the common pattern. The unwritten law of conformity results in one of the outstanding differences between the American college student and his European counterpart. Europeans, especially the intellectuals, want to differ in every respect from their fellow-men. European college students, also, believe that everything from dresses and hairsets to literary, artistic and musical appreciation should have an individual touch. Contradict, try to be unique, then you will be considered "individual," then you have "personality."

But in the U.S.A., to be different among adults as well as among adolescents is to be queer, odd, unpopular. And popularity is after all something which most Americans are craving for. Especially college students! [1]

Generally speaking, the refugee scholar experienced considerable difficulty in adjusting his standard of living so that it would conform to the relatively lower income which he could command in the United States. When he had a wife and children to support, he found going particularly hard. *Refugees in America* indirectly compares American and European professional life:

The European housewife, less accustomed than her American counterpart to doing her own work, was surprised and sometimes vocal about the scarcity and high cost of domestic help. European husbands, after the first shock of seeing American professors help their wives wash the dishes, mind the baby, sweep the rugs, and put up the screens, soon found they had to learn to fit into the routine themselves, since in America college professors' salaries are far from munificent. Displaced scholars, like other refugees, were struck by the fact that, although the general standard of living in the United States is quite high, middle-class professional incomes are not such as to make possible much more than a relatively simple style of existence. [2]

If the institution to which the scholar was called was situated in a large city, rent and living expenses would inevitably

---

[1] Erna Barschak, *My American Adventure* (New York: Ives Washburn, 1945), pp. 107, 113–114.

[2] Maurice R. Davie, *et al.*, *Refugees in America* (New York: Harper & Brothers, 1947), p. 309.

be high. It is true that this disadvantage was sometimes bal-
anced by opportunities to write paid articles for periodicals
or to deliver lectures on subjects within his special field or
more popularly upon conditions in Nazi Europe. Such opportunities were less readily cultivated when the college or university was located in a small town or rural community, but,
outside the urban setting, costs of living tended to be lower
and chances of settling down into the American milieu were
immeasurably greater. Typical of the point of view of many
refugees is this statement taken from an interview with a
Polish scholar:

He believed that scholars in general had made a very good
adjustment here. They liked the atmosphere of the little college
towns, he declared, preferring them to the hustle and bustle of
the big cities. He himself liked Riverdale much better than New
York City proper. Scholars should put their roots down in
American life, and he insisted that they could best do this in
the small towns. What the scholars had brought with them had
had its inspiration in the Old World. It would in time dry up,
and they must have new sources on which to draw.

The chances of placement were few for scholars unacquainted with the use of English, inasmuch as ours is a
non-linguistic people unfamiliar with foreign languages. Acquaintance with and mastery of a second tongue are two
separate and distinct things. Henry Sigerist has feelingly
expressed the chasm which yawns between one's mother
tongue and an acquired language:

The language in which we uttered our first words, in which
we expressed our emotions, in which we formulated our thoughts
and developed our own style, has become an essential part of
our personality. Only those who have gone through the experience know that feeling of humiliating helplessness and frustra-
tion that a mature scholar feels when all of a sudden he has to
carry on his work in a foreign tongue and know how much time

it takes before he is able to express himself in his own personal style in the new language.[3]

Professor Eduard Heimann relates this problem closely to the requirements of the teaching profession:

The mental obstacles to the process of adjustment center on the problem of language. Without a personal transplantation, only professional philologists can be fully aware of the deep-reaching implications which are entailed by familiarity with one language instead of with another. In the new country all become aroused to a sense of this vital issue, whether as salesmen or waiters or anything else. It is, however, teachers and writers who most conspicuously toil under this specter which haunts their days and nights; and in them it is best studied, not as a special problem but as the most marked example of a problem typical of all.[4]

It would sometimes happen that the head of the family acquired facility in English before his wife and young children felt at home in the new language. Under these circumstances, adjustment of the entire family was likely to be retarded. In large cities with foreign-speaking communities of considerable size the scholar and his family might happily rejoin friends known formerly in Europe or make new acquaintances among their own language group; but the refugee who settled in a rural community was often thrown with residents unfamiliar with and hostile to foreigners. Moreover, it would be idle to pretend that he did not occasionally meet with discrimination. Fortunate were those scholars who entered sections of the country whose cultural heritage had nurtured a strong tradition of hospitality. An excerpt from a communication from a refugee teacher states:

---

[3] "Epistola Dedicatoria," by Henry Sigerist, in Celebration of the Seventieth Birthday of Arturo Castiglioni, *Yale Journal of Biology and Medicine*, Vol. 17, No. 2 (Dec., 1944), p. 415.

[4] Eduard Heimann, "The Refugee Speaks," *Annals of the American Academy of Political and Social Science*, Vol. 203 (1939), p. 111.

We feel that we have been very fortunate in living in a place like Haverford. I have never seen people who took so much interest in other people. I don't know whether it's because we are refugees or not, but certainly everyone has been extraordinarily kind to us and interested in us. You take when our last baby was born. We were given a shower which we never knew anything about till it came. Then we joined a Friends Meeting not so long ago. When the last child was born we found that the Meeting wanted very much to contribute to our expenses. I didn't like to take anything at all, but the money was sent anonymously. Now I have to pay the Meeting back! It is really amazing how friendly people are. Of course not all Americans are quite this way, but people here do seem to have tremendous interest to really help others in every way. It is a very happy asset to American life not found in Germany. I don't think it's particularly Haverford, we found the same kind of people in Vermont.

To the everlasting credit of American scholars it should be said that they usually extended a hearty and sympathetic welcome to their colleagues from overseas, assisting them in their orientation to American academic life and sharing with them social contacts with the help of which their adaptation to the new environment was hastened. As an investigator who made a survey of American educational institutions for the Emergency Committee in 1939 put it, "Faculty members with whom I have talked all agree with me that American teachers have a moral obligation to help their fellows who are victims of the current insanity in Europe." That members of the academic community throughout the world felt a similar compulsion was borne out by Walter M. Kotschnig several years earlier:

Incidentally it is interesting to note that of the 6,000–7,000 professional workers with university training who left Germany, the university teachers, though by no means all of them obtained new positions, found it on the whole easier than other professional groups to continue their work in foreign countries. The way they were received and helped by their foreign colleagues is proof that at least in one field of human endeavour international solidarity and the realization of the oneness of learning prevailed over nationalist conceptions and the narrow economic interests.[5]

Professors and their wives made unusual efforts towards this objective. Though this attitude was evident in an over-whelming number of cases, the bitterness of isolation was expressed by one scholar who said:

I still feel like a foreigner . . . and it is the same way with my colleagues at Yale, Columbia, and Harvard. Although we are accepted as faculty members, we are not accepted as Americans even though we have had our citizenship papers for some time. We are still foreigners in the eyes of those about us, and foreigners we shall remain to the end of the chapter.

This sense of not-belonging, and a nostalgic yearning for the homeland which persisted in spite of efforts towards integration in the new community, were aggravated by anxiety about relatives left behind in Europe. One professor wrote, voicing the experience of many:

The years have, naturally, been difficult ones. In addition to the necessity of an adjustment to a new environment, new methods of teaching and new material, the development in Europe has influenced us greatly, as the father of my wife was deported by the Nazis and as we did not hear from him [he died in the camp] and other members of our families for years.

Certain scholars lost all track of wives and children, and went on year after year with no sure knowledge of whether they lived or had perished. To some among them, a long period of uncertainty was terminated by a report of the extermination of those nearest and dearest to them.

As has already been made evident, some professors suc-

---

[5] Walter M. Kotschnig, *Unemployment in the Learned Professions* (London: Oxford University Press, 1937), p. 226.

ceeded in bringing into the United States members of their families. This was not possible without a severe strain upon meager financial resources, as one scholar made clear:

> After the Nazi pogroms of November, 1938, I was forced to help out from Germany the brother of my father and his wife; my uncle had been taken to a concentration camp and was released only when I sent temporary visas for Panama for himself and his wife. Since, in consequence of the Nazi regulations for Jewish emigrants, he arrived penniless, I had to support the two persons during their stay in Panama for more than six months; I also paid the fee for their visas, amounting to $170. Furthermore my mother found herself forced to leave Germany early this year and to come to Panama where she is now waiting for her immigration visa for the United States. She also entirely depends on me.

Even where immigrant families were united in the new homeland, the lot of the scholar's wife might be unenviable. This is a man's world, and the woman who accompanies her husband into exile must leave much of her own life behind her. In Dr. Sigerist's pointed words:

> We, after all, have our books and when we have books we can do our work wherever we happen to be. A wife misses her relatives, her friends, the comforts of her former home, the infinity of little things that make life pleasant, much more than we, and there is much greater heroism in her unspectacular adjustment.[6]

Nearly always it was found that the children of displaced scholars became thoroughly adjusted to their new surroundings. Colloquial English they learned from other children, while grammatical English came to them readily in the public schools which most of them attended. Refugee children en-

---

[6] Henry Sigerist, *ibid.,* p. 416.

tered into the strenuous life of the high school with enthusiasm. The college in which the displaced scholar was invited to teach inclined to be generous toward his children, frequently accepting those of college age as students with remission of fees. Children of displaced scholars who were attached to an institution in a city often found outlets, on reaching maturity, in the business and industrial life of the community. The grown-up children of the scholar at a college in a small town had greater difficulty in securing a foothold and might be obliged to leave the new home to make their way in urban areas. The records abound in touching and heart-warming stories of the younger members of refugee scholars' families. Dorothy Jones wrote in the *Detroit News*, March 14, 1943, of the daughter of an Emergency Committee scholar:

A little girl whose first name is known to engineers all over the world feels that she paid part of a big debt to America a few days ago when she won the fifth grade Detroit News Spelling Bee championship at Duane Doty School. . . .

Three years ago, when Involut Vogel left her home and playmates in Berlin, Germany, to come to America she couldn't speak a word of English. A week ago last Friday she spelled down all the American children in her grade. Involut, a happy little girl with sparkling blue eyes and long curls, could tell Americans a lot about their country.

Another account tells of the young son of a refugee scholar who, some little while after he had picked up English, won an oratorical contest and became, after six years, the top high-school scientist in the country, winning first honors in the National Science Talent Search.

The two sons of another exiled professor were nominated the "most brilliant members" of their graduating class at Princeton University.

A scholar writing to the Committee during the war years might have been any American parent telling about his children:

My son was inducted into the Army last June, then had his basic training, Infantry, at Camp Croft, which made it possible for him, until recently, to spend once in a while a week end here with me. Last Saturday he left for a California Port of Embarcation. I had only one letter from him since his arrival there, and don't know as yet what his next assignment is going to be. My youngest daughter is still at the University. She will be a Junior on March the first (rather young, only 18, she makes excellent records) and is planning to go on at least until July, that means to finish her first Junior semester. We shall then decide whether she shall go on studying or, as she is planning now, work for some time; the costs of living in the University towns are getting higher and higher, and my salary is rather small for times like the present ones, and I can also feel how much more one has to spend if he doesn't live in a home. It thus becomes harder and harder, to take care of two persons; I don't like the idea, though, of her giving up her studies, just one year before finishing; for if she went right on, in July, she could become a senior in November and graduate in July 1945.

So thoroughly convinced did many refugee scholars become of the benefits which would accrue to their children in the American scene, that they nearly always expressed their intention to remain in the United States for their children's sake even though postwar conditions in Europe should make possible a return to their homeland.

INFLUENCE OF THE FOREIGN SCHOLAR

If the unfamiliar environment in which the displaced foreign scholar found himself had a profound influence upon him and his family, a few words must be said concerning his own influence upon the new environment.

It is no disparagement of the American university or college professor to say that the foreign professor in a university situated in one of the great countries of Western civilization is usually more exacting than his American counterpart in his demands upon his students in the matter of research. This is perhaps best illustrated by the difference that exists in France between the degree of *Doctorat d'état* and *Doctorat de l'université*. The former degree is seldom secured by a French scholar before he is thirty-five years of age, and usually not until he is older. The dissertation is the result of mature study, investigation, and reflection upon his subject. It is seldom a brochure or a small book, but is very often a profound study and a real contribution to the subject. The philosopher Henri Bergson was forty-eight when he published his thesis for the Doctorat d'état, "Creative Evolution." The Doctorat de l'université, on the other hand, was organized for the benefit of foreign students who enter French universities with the expectation of securing a degree comparable to our Ph.D. and getting it in comparable time—that is, in two or three years. It is not suggested that the Doctorat de l'université is granted as the result of superficial scholarship. It is mentioned because the possession of the Doctorat d'état by a professor would mean a demand upon the part of its possessor of a high degree of meticulous scholarship from his students. There may have been at times a lack of imagination but not of precision. Scholarly exactitude was well illustrated in the University in Exile (of which we shall have more to say later), where a number of German, French and Belgian displaced scholars taught as the result of grants made by the Emergency Committee or by the Rockefeller Foundation. They soon published monographs of superior merit which made a deep impression upon their students and upon American scholars generally.

The great majority of the displaced scholars were, moreover, men of general culture who added *urbanitas* to the institution and to the community in which it was situated. This was particularly true when the foreign scholar was placed in a college in a small town. A professor of mathematics might become very popular in the community because of his ability to talk upon art or literature. One foreign professor in a small institution organized a choir and an orchestra from among the students which soon roused great enthusiasm in the community, an enthusiasm which was rapidly extended to neighboring districts. He made his institution a center of cultural influence in that field, and music knows no limitations of nationality. An economist wrote us of his avocational interests:

As an experienced cellist and ensemble player, I have established for myself a reputation in the state and have guided students' activities in the field: by forming ensemble groups (instrumental and vocal) on the campus, to whom I introduced the priceless treasures of European secular and sacred music especially adapted for smaller ensembles (Collegium Musicum).

Another refugee scholar made available musical recordings and accompanying lectures for army hospitals as part of the readjustment program for wounded soldiers. One musicologist found time after his classes were over to lecture on musical subjects before groups of interested club members, write numerous articles for the press and musical publications, and talk over the radio, often on Mozart, about whom he was an authority. Many were the free addresses given on Islamic art, medieval stained glass, ancient Greek costume, theater design, the art of the dance, Indo-European linguistics, and other subjects, before adult audiences in libraries and museums. These lectures were sometimes given before audiences of the scholars' own language groups who were for the moment out of touch with intellectual life in the new country because of initial difficulties with its speech. The versatility and adaptability of these scholars was noteworthy, as in the case of the professor who wrote:

I soon was asked to help in the educational and religious work of the School of Theology which is training the ministers for the German-speaking Congregational churches of America. In addition to my position as head of the German department I became a member of the faculty of the School of Theology and I gave courses in history of German thought, the German Bible and in hymnology. I often was invited by German-speaking churches of the surrounding states to serve as a minister for special occasions. I have enjoyed this part of my work especially, because it gave me the opportunity to work for a deeper international understanding.

The Emergency Committee cooperated with the most important libraries of the country, especially the Library of Congress and the New York Public Library. It supported five displaced scholars engaged in a unique and noteworthy piece of research in collaboration with Archibald MacLeish and the staff of the Library of Congress. Mr. MacLeish wrote of them:

They have done much important work for the Library; but their particular assignment has been to survey and evaluate the collections. These surveys make it possible for me to know in considerable detail what, in the opinion of these specialists, the Library of Congress needs.

In the New York Public Library, the Emergency Committee assisted six scholars of specialized ability. In a letter to Dr. Duggan dated September 26, 1945, Franklin F. Hopper, Director of the Library, stated:

Dr. Roman Jakobson, widely known in academic circles as a scholar specializing in general linguistics, especially phonetics, in Slavic philology and in Paleo-Asiatic languages, completed for the Library a valuable study of Aleutian manuscript material from the point of view of language and folklore.

Dr. Aron Freimann, a leading bibliographer of our day, whose extraordinary achievements in Hebrew bibliography have given him universal recognition as a first rank authority on Hebrew manuscripts and printed books and on the history of Hebrew printing, completed for the Library a much needed book in Hebrew bibliography, namely, a gazetteer of Hebrew printings from the 15th century to the present day with a masterly survey of the history of Hebrew printing. In addition he compiled a complete bibliographical record of all known extant manuscripts of the writings of Rashi, a 12th century Franco-Jewish scholar; and also has collected data on Jewish incunabula printed in Roman characters.

Dr. Franz Rapp did important work in the Theatre Collection checking, identifying, systematizing, and indexing material, as well as making bibliographical researches of a higher order.

Mr. Simon Lissim has given free courses in decorative and applied art for children at several of the branches and gave also an evening class for adults. The classes proved of real value in educational and cultural development.

Dr. Kathe Meyer-Baer's remarkable musical knowledge was a great aid to our Music Division in identifying Chopin first editions and in analyzing 16th century music.

Dr. Adolf Leo Oppenheim prepared a catalogue of the Sumerian texts which the Library had secured from Wilberforce Eames. This catalogue was published by the American Oriental Society.

It would be pleasant to assume that, coincident with the general success which characterized the personal and professional relations of the group as a whole, every displaced scholar was possessed of a charm of manner and equable temperament which enabled him to make an easy and happy adjustment to the community in which he found himself. It can scarcely diminish the stature of the group, however, to admit that even in so distinguished a gathering as those outstanding professors and scientists who came to the United

States during the 1930's, with or without the help of the Emergency Committee, a small number found difficulty in fitting into the new environment. Such instances were the exception. A few—a very few—scholars exhibited too openly the condescension which the scholarship and mores of their American colleagues inspired in them. Occasionally they were critical of one another:

"The difficulty with Dr. X.," commented one observer, "is that his ambitions are greater than his actual adaptation to an English-speaking environment. His relations to the other members of that . . . group of well educated refugees . . . appear to be strained."

"Y. is not very practical," a friendly colleague admitted, "not a good mixer, not an attractive speaker (in English— though not a bad one either) nor altogether a captivating personality. At the same time I have to this day the same high opinion of his culture and scholarship and character."

The wording of the following excerpt from a letter written in 1941 has been very slightly recast to prevent identification:

Dr. Z. has been very successful in his lectures which were just the type of lectures for small-town people. Dr. Z. had a very hard time to adjust himself outside these lectures but in the last weeks found contact with the local people and both he and Mrs. Z. were liked by most of them. Part of his difficulties is due to his nervousness . . . The students who sometimes really liked him, used to say: Dr. Z. has two natures, and the director, having watched twice when he lost his last bit of self-restraint and yelled at a colleague, agrees to this opinion. The Z.'s hardly mixed with the college people . . . Furthermore, they spoke constantly German and that was resented by the students . . . He is, moreover, very critical of American taste and customs.

A small number gave offense to administrative officers by their very anxiety and lack of feeling of security. Driven by fear of the future, and goaded on by the importunings of wives less versed than they in American academic ways, they would occasionally—and understandably—nag the college administration for positive assurance as to the date and manner in which they would be added to the permanent faculty. At a time when pay cuts had not yet been restored to all American faculty members, these requests for reassurance were not always sympathetically received.

There were a few tragic cases of utter inability to adjust to the local environment. Some scholars, on the other hand, met their Waterloo in such specific situations as their inability to satisfy the needs of undergraduate students. A college president wrote of one such scholar:

> His work with the students is characterized by a great "remoteness." Personally a gentle and likable man, he is not disinterested but simply oblivious to any relationship between himself and the students. It is doubtful that he would ever develop into an undergraduate teacher, although as a research worker he would probably do a brilliant job judged from the standpoint of the European savant—deficient, however, according to American standards.

> Last year he conducted an extracurricular seminar. Here he enjoyed real success. The more mature members of his audience said that they got a great deal out of his discussions—although they had to go more than two-thirds of the way themselves. The usual Master's candidate would probably not benefit.

Death took its toll of the displaced scholars. To be driven from the land of one's fathers, often after having been robbed of all one's possessions, and then to have to face the making of a new life in a distant country, where a strange tongue was spoken and strange customs prevailed, was veritable hardship for a mature scholar. When in addition the standard of living for himself and his family fell and a sense of insecurity was naggingly present, the gradual breakdown in physical and sometimes mental health upon the part of a few can readily be understood.

It was nonetheless a shock to receive the following letter from the dean of one of our colleges:

28 March 1944

DEAR DR. DUGGAN:

It grieves me very much to inform you that Dr.   took his own life when he was suffering a period of depression that was unbearable to him. I have been unable to discover any very evident immediate cause of this tragedy. Dr.   had made many friends here, had entered into the activities of the campus, was getting ahead with his writing, and was assured of a position at the college for the coming year. He maintained a cheerful manner with students and colleagues, but it was known to a few intimates and to his physician that he was deeply disturbed in spirit. I can think only that his prolonged bitter experiences and suffering finally overwhelmed his so sensitive nature.

Despite the hardships suffered by many of our own grantees, there were only two instances of suicide among them.

In the twelve and more years of the Committee's life, some twenty-six of its grantees and Fellows died. In view of the mental stress and physical strain which was so frequently the refugees' lot, it is not surprising that a number of these deaths were due to aggravated cardiac conditions. A statement follows concerning each scholar who died. We offer tribute to the memory of these fine men and women whose careers were in many cases shortened by the adversities they endured. Brief though these identifying notes are, they speak eloquently of the outstanding character of the group with whom the work of the Emergency Committee was associated.

Dr. Hans Beutler, physicist, whose work in Europe with the Kaiser Wilhelm Institute for Physical Chemistry in Berlin and with the University of Berlin was followed by association in this country with the University of Michigan and the University of Chicago, died in December, 1942.

Theodor Brauer, internationally known in the field of labor problems, died in March, 1942, while a professor of economics at the College of St. Thomas in St. Paul, Minnesota.

Warner F. Brook, professor of economics at the New School for Social Research, whose experience with problems of price control and regulation of raw materials provided a rich background for study of situations arising out of World War II, had enjoyed guest appointments at both the University of Kansas City and the University of Wisconsin before his death in 1945.

Ernst Cohn-Wiener, whose long career as an orientalist included an appointment as Director of Art in Baroda State, India, died in 1941 while a member of the faculty of the Iranian Institute in New York City.

Eva Fiesel, renowned authority on the Etruscan language, who had been absorbed by Bryn Mawr College, died in May, 1937, in the midst of preparation of her Etruscan dictionary.

Julius Fischer, whose rich experience in municipal administration abroad had included an appointment as commissioner of housing in a city of Austria, was engaged in writing a study of housing cooperatives from the viewpoint of the housing needs of American families in the moderate income brackets at the time of his death in 1943.

Hans Fried, Viennese mathematician, rendered service as assistant in the Sproul Observatory, and later as lecturer in mathematics at Swarthmore College, until his death in December, 1945.

Felix M. Gatz, who from 1923 to 1933 headed the Berlin Philharmonic Orchestra in the concerts of the Bruckner Society, died in 1942 after eight years in this country, during which he taught music and aesthetics at Duquesne University, New York University, St. John's University, and the University of Scranton.

Moritz Geiger, who had himself once studied at Harvard University during his years as a Privatdozent, and whose classes later when he was a professor at Göttingen attracted both philosophers and mathematicians, found a congenial working place at Vassar College. His last summer was devoted to his work on aesthetics, which was nearing completion at the time of his death in September, of 1937.[7]

Werner Hegemann, international authority on town planning who was credited with a major part in the elimination of Berlin slums, had practiced architecture in the United States during the First World War. In New York following Hitler's rise to power he taught at the New School for Social Research and Columbia University. He died in April, 1936.

Victor Jollos, whose career as a zoologist in Europe had included appointments at the University of Berlin, the Kaiser Wilhelm Institute for Biology, and the University of Edinburgh, taught at the University of Wisconsin where he was a grantee of the Committee during 1933–1935. His death occurred in July, 1941.

Fritz Lehmann, economist, formerly of the University of Cologne, was professor of money and banking in the Graduate Faculty of Political and Social Science of the New School for Social Research in New York. He was active in this country as a writer and lecturer on monetary problems, credit, and banking. He died in 1940.

Kurt Lewin, psychologist, formerly of the University of Berlin, died on February 12, 1947. Since his immigration to the United States, he had been professor at Stanford, at Cornell, and at the University of Iowa, and at the time of his death was Director of the Research Center for Group Dynamics at Massachusetts Institute of Technology. He had also

---

[7] Ralph Barton Perry, *Moritz Geiger*, an address given at a memorial service in the Vassar College Chapel, Dec. 7, 1937.

taught at Harvard University and the University of California. During World War II, Dr. Lewin served with the Office of Strategic Services.

Moritz Löwi, psychologist, formerly professor at the University of Breslau, taught at Connecticut College for Women and served in a Norwich hospital before his death in January, 1944.

Emmy Noether, "a great mathematician . . . who changed the face of algebra by her work," [8] passed away at the height of her powers in April, 1935, while a member of the faculty at Bryn Mawr College.

Alexander Haim Pekelis, distinguished legal mind, perished in an airplane crash near Shannon Airport, Eire, in December, 1946, when on his way back to the United States from Switzerland, where he had been a delegate of American Labor Zionists at a World Zionist Congress. Dr. Pekelis was the first foreign-born editor of the *Columbia Law Review*.

George Petschek, for many years professor of law at the University of Vienna and since 1938 research associate in law at Harvard University, died on September 5, 1947, at the age of seventy-five.

Richard Prager, formerly professor of astronomy at the University of Berlin, and a leading authority on the history and bibliography of variable stars, was attached to Harvard University at the time of his death in July, 1945.

Arthur Rosenberg, formerly professor of history at the University of Berlin, scholarly expert on the German Republic, was a member of the faculty at Brooklyn College until his death in February, 1943.

Hans Rosenberg, astronomer, who had come from a professorship at the University of Kiel, returned to the Old

---

[8] Hermann Weyl, *Emmy Noether* (New York: Scripta Mathematica, 1935).

World after a number of years at the Yerkes Observatory in this country. He became Director of the Observatory in Istanbul, and died in that city in 1940.

Martin Sommerfeld, noted Germanist and literary historian from the University of Frankfurt, had been associated with Smith College, Columbia University, New York University, College of the City of New York, and Queens College before his death in July, 1939.

Hugo Steiner-Prag, a professor at the Leipzig State Academy of Art and one-time president of the Association of German Book Illustrators which he helped establish, served as professor of graphic arts at New York University after his arrival in the United States, and acted as consultant on book design for the University of Nebraska Press and the Book-of-the-Month Club. His death occurred in September, 1945.

William Stern, the illustrious psychologist, former director of the Psychological Institute of Hamburg, became professor at Duke University and in 1936 was one of the distinguished scholars invited from thirty universities throughout the world to teach in the Harvard Tercentenary Summer School. He died in March, 1938.

Veit Valentin, exiled German historian, died on January 12, 1947. Formerly professor at the University of Freiburg, Dr. Valentin had been director of the Reichsarchiv, the official collection of historical documents. Associated in this country with the Fletcher School of Law and Diplomacy at Tufts College, and with the Library of Congress, Dr. Valentin devoted himself to the study of the 1848 migration of Germans to this country. According to the *New York Times*, after the Nazi surrender he went to Germany for the Office of Strategic Services to examine captured documents.

Edgar Zilsel, distinguished Viennese philosopher, was a

member of the faculty of Mills College at the time of his death in March, 1944.

Heinrich Zimmer, formerly professor at the University of Heidelberg, well known as a philosopher and specialist in comparative religion, was associated with Columbia University prior to his death in March, 1943.

CHAPTER IV

The Displaced Scholar and the War Effort

BEFORE the United States entered the war, American scientists had assessed the contributions which their refugee colleagues could make to the national defense. Realization of their potential value was increasing. Professor R. A. Gortner of the University of Minnesota wrote to Dr. Duggan in June, 1941, of convictions which he had held for many years:

> I firmly believe that we could reduce the technological achievement of Central Europe to the basis of a technological achievement of Spain and Portugal if we could move out 1,000 of their strategic men who are leaders in the field of natural sciences, and in the long run the battle for democracy would be won more cheaply by doing just this and the results would be much more permanent than can ever be accomplished by the billions of dollars which we are pouring into our own defense program. Only a minor amount of the defense funds would need to be earmarked for such a program and we as a nation would gain immeasurably not only in intellectual power but also in material welfare. . . .
>
> Fritz Haber is an example of what I mean. He and he alone kept Germany in the First World War after the first year had elapsed. Without his process for the manufacture of synthetic nitrogen from the air the First World War would never have been fought. Fritz Haber fled to Switzerland and died there a suicide. Had we been able to bring Fritz Haber to the United States we would have scored a major victory.

Herbert Freundlich of the Kaiser Wilhelm Institute at Berlin was another example of the First World War. Without his studies which enabled the Germans to protect their armies in gas warfare gas would never have been introduced in the first place, and had it been introduced the German armies would have been decimated when the gas manufacturing facilities of the United States were thrown on the scales. For this he was rewarded by Hitler with essential banishment.

Other examples of the type of people that I have in mind are Professor George B. Kistiakowsky at the present time professor of chemistry at Harvard University who came to the United States in 1926, Professor Peter Debye who has just taken over the headship of the chemistry department at Cornell University, Albert Einstein at the Institute for Advanced Study, etc. The list could be expanded very largely, but I believe the illustrations which I have already used are adequate.

In spite of need strongly felt in many quarters, however, it was not until we were in actual combat that foreign displaced scientists who had sought refuge in the United States came fully into their own. The discriminating words of Dr. Bruzs of Latvia, in his 1938 report to the Committee on Science and its Social Relations of the International Council of Scientific Unions, come to mind: "I distinguish two elements in science, its utility and its intellectual charm." [1] In the smoke of battle, nations are understandably less preoccupied with the charms of science than with its usefulness. Whereas for years lack of laboratory facilities or need of a job with which to keep body and soul together had often prevented the refugee intellectual from pursuing the delights of his calling suddenly he was called upon to mobilize his knowledge for the national welfare.

On December 7, 1941, came the Japanese attack upon

---

[1] Quoted in Walter B. Cannon and Richard M. Field, "International Relations in Science," *Chronica Botanica*, Vol. 9, No. 4 (Autumn, 1945), pp. 285–286.

Pearl Harbor, and with it the entrance of the United States into World War II. Now the displaced scholar had his opportunity to contribute to the war effort of his adopted country in the classroom, in government bureaus, at the proving grounds, or in the laboratory.

Participation in the war effort affected every one of our economic and social institutions; but upon none of these did it exert a more profound or far-reaching influence than upon American colleges and universities. Here changes in plant and structure became inevitable, the number and kind of students were altered, perplexing problems in management confronted harassed administrations, and curricula had to be tailored to meet war needs. Almost all male students nineteen years of age and over were enrolled in the army, navy, or marines. Others received instruction in revised courses of training which placed strong emphasis upon the scientific and technical branches of learning as a preparation for the war effort. "Accelerated" programs to guarantee an early supply of technical assistants were introduced. There was strong emphasis upon the faculties of medicine and language, whose graduates were in special demand, but no technical field was overlooked.

All these factors had their effect upon the refugee scholar. Younger American teachers in colleges and universities were drawn into the army and navy, while older instructors in the scientific and technical faculties were drafted by the military services for research on special problems of defense and offense. For a time many institutions found themselves all but denuded of mathematicians, physicists, and chemists. It was natural and inevitable that the ranks should be filled up by displaced scholars. By 1941, many of the newcomers had become American citizens, and although the military authorities were reluctant to employ recently naturalized men and women upon technical jobs of secret character, exceptions were made if unusual skill, appropriate experience, and an unblemished security record had peculiarly qualified the refugee for the work which was to be done. Here at long last the displaced scholar stood among his peers, accepted as one of them. Paradoxically enough, it was in the rush and fever of implementing accelerated programs and specialized training courses, that displaced intellectuals found themselves in a more nearly normal working situation than they could have hoped to find in peacetime. As one college administrator stated, what was expected of refugees was no more and no less than what would have been expected of Americans in comparable jobs. And émigré scholars responded handsomely to the demands made upon them.

The interest of friendly administrators among the defense services in the work of the Emergency Committee is reflected in the following letter written to Dr. Duggan on March 2, 1942, by Dr. Robert Leigh, former president of Bennington College:

I am working with the National Resources Planning Board, and one of my tasks is to serve as an executive in connection with the Science Committee of the Board. This Committee is made up of representatives of the National Research Council, the Social Science Research Council, and others.

At the last meeting of this Committee there was a discussion of the loss of scientific and scholarly help due to the regulations which prevent qualified and loyal alien scholars from carrying on business tasks for the government. It was left to me to find out the facts regarding the regulations and to see what forces are afoot to get some reasonable individual relaxation of the barriers.

It occurred to me that you might be in a position to give me a description of what is being done and has been done, and who is working on the problem. I am not at all sure that the Science Committee can or will do anything, but I want to find out what the possibilities are.

The information provided by the Committee stimulated increased use of our refugee scholars.

A report of the Committee's grantees and Fellows as of June 30, 1944, during the progress of the war, showed that thirty-one of its scholars were employed with government bureaus, including the Office of Strategic Services, the Bureau of Economic Warfare, the Office of War Information, and the Office of Price Administration. Eighty-seven other grantees were engaged in some other form of activity helpful to the war effort, ranging from contributions of time and service to the Office of Civilian Defense and donations of plasma to the blood banks, to participation as teachers in the Army Specialized Training Program, Navy V-12 Program, Civil Affairs Training Schools and Allied Military Government classes. Several answered that they had worked with commissions studying the location of cultural monuments within occupied Europe so that these monuments might be spared during bombing raids. One had worked with the International Labour Office in Montreal, and another was engaged in teaching classes for the Canadian Army Corps. Five served on the Applied Mathematics Panel for the National Defense Research Council. One lectured on musicology at an army hospital as part of the recreational readjustment program. Two former scholars were employed as mathematicians at the Aberdeen Proving Ground in Maryland. Several had temporarily left academic posts to devote all their time to war work. One scholar wrote that he had given up the teaching of art history in order to work in the engineering department of a large shipyard as draftsman. A chemist was working on a portable still for use in life rafts so that sea water might be made potable. A malacologist contributed information about such edible or poisonous invertebrate animals as the army might expect to encounter in out-of-the-way corners of the globe.

Scholars wrote not only about themselves but about their children as well, a number of whom were in the armed forces. A former grantee remarked: "One boy of mine is in the air corps, another is an already disabled war veteran, a third will go to the army now." The son of another was in the Navy. One of the scholars told of a son who was in active service as an intelligence officer overseas. Typical was the letter from a former grantee written in 1946 which stated proudly: "My son took part in the Pacific campaign from Bougainville over New Guinea, Leyte landing, Manila, to Japan, and last October, has been discharged with eighty-six points. He is not yet quite twenty-one, and at present a student of the University."

Supporters of the Emergency Committee have sometimes said, half in earnest, half in jest, that the Emergency Committee in Aid of Displaced Foreign Scholars imported the atomic bomb. This is friendly if gross exaggeration: although many of Europe's noted atomic physicists who were obliged to flee because of racial or political reasons turned to the Committee for help, most of them made their own contacts in this country and were successful in securing scientific appointments independently of this organization's help. Yet the Committee's rôle need not be minimized, for much assistance was given, through correspondence and letters of introduction, to a number of Europe's displaced men of science who worked on the applications of nuclear fission. Of the Committee's grantees and Fellows, five were atomic physicists, and at least two were known to have been active in research in the United States on atomic energy for military purposes: one the Nobel Prize Laureate, James Franck, a director in the Metallurgical Project; the other the Italian physicist, Bruno Rossi, who worked at Los Alamos Laboratory on an important phase of the experimental program connected with the engineering of the atomic bomb. There is some reason to believe that as security regulations lift, it will be found that others among the Committee's former grantees, as well as among scholars less directly aided by the Committee, contributed to the working out of the Manhattan Project. It is significant that the Official Report on the development of the atomic bomb under the auspices of the United States Government contains this statement: "At that time [January, 1939] American-born nuclear physicists were so unaccustomed to the idea of using their science for military purposes that they hardly realized what needed to be done. Consequently the early efforts both at restricting publication and at getting government support were stimulated largely by a small group of foreign-born physicists centering on L. Szilard and including E. Wigner, E. Teller, V. F. Weisskopf, and E. Fermi." [2]

One way or another, the hopes and expectations of Professor Gortner, and of others like him, were realized by the time of the war's end. Even before R. G. D. Richardson declared in 1944 that there were more of the leading German mathematicians in the United States than there were in Germany, no less a personage than Grand Admiral Karl Doenitz, in a letter to the German scientist, Professor Karl Kuepfmueller, written December 14, 1943, deplored the scientific impoverishment of the Reich. In speaking of U-boat warfare he is reported to have stated,

For some months past, the enemy has rendered the U-boat war ineffective. He has achieved this objective, not through superior tactics or strategy but through his superiority in the field of science; this finds its expression in the modern battle weapon, detection. By this means, he has torn our sole offensive weapon

[2] Henry De Wolf Smyth, *Atomic Energy for Military Purposes: The Official Report on the Development of the Atomic Bomb Under the Auspices of the United States Government, 1940–1945* (Princeton: Princeton Univ. Press, 1946), p. 45.

in the war against the Anglo-Saxons from our hands. It is essential to victory that we make good our scientific disparity and thereby restore to the U-boat its fighting qualities.[3]

It was not only in the scientific and technical fields of learning that the refugee scholar proved his worth. He was especially needed in the field of languages. A scholar of the Committee wrote, "During the war I conducted, assisted by natives of India, a number of very successful courses on Hindustani in connection with the war effort." Another told us, "I wrote for the American Council of Learned Societies the army manual of Spoken Greek." While military authorities placed little value on the study of the literature of a foreign language and small emphasis upon the study of its grammar and structure, they badly needed men and women who could speak the language itself. An ability to read and write it was also valuable, but the need for our officers to talk with the natives of the overrun countries, and especially of Germany and Japan, was of the first importance. The refugee scholar was sometimes the best instructor in the accelerated teaching of foreign languages and especially of German.

In still another endeavor of the military authorities the refugee scholar was of almost unique value. The army knew that when the day of victory arrived, it would be its task to take over the administration of Germany. To do this with any measure of success it would be necessary to have a reservoir on which to draw, of personnel familiar with the geography, history, government, and forms of administration of Germany, but especially with the psychology of the German people. No person was better qualified to prepare Americans for this task than the refugee scholar. He was thoroughly familiar with the German *Kultur* of pre-Hitler days and knew

---

[3] Letter released by Rear Admiral H. G. Bowen, Chief of the Navy's Office of Research and Inventions, *New York Times*, Feb. 14, 1946.

from sad personal experience the meaning of the Nazi totalitarian ideology. In the special schools organized by the military authorities for the training of men and women as administrators in Germany after victory, the refugee scholar was of unusual value as a teacher. This was equally true of the school established at the University of Maryland for the training of assistants in the work to be undertaken by the United Nations Relief and Rehabilitation Administration in the devastated areas. Two of the Committee's former stipendiaries taught at Biarritz American University in 1946, while a former scholar, Dr. R. M. W. Kempner, was attached as Deputy Chief of Counsel to the legal staff prosecuting major Axis war criminals in the Nuremberg trials.

This has been part of the record of the Committee's men and women in the war effort. There is still a large contribution which they can make to the new homeland. With the settling down to the struggles and conflicts of a peacetime world, the active rôle of the scientist and scholar does not end. What science has labored to destroy, it must now dedicate itself to rebuild. There is ample room for the gifts of all intellectuals, refugees and natives alike. As Thomas B. Appleget has so strongly put it:

If there is any nucleus of international goodwill and understanding left in the world, it resides, I think, in scientific personnel. They will be the first to mend the broken wires of communication, and I hope this time all the world will realize, whether we like it or not, we have to live together on a globe which science has made too small for war.[4]

---

[4] Quoted in Walter B. Cannon and Richard M. Field, *ibid.*, p. 258.

CHAPTER V

The Emergency Committee Completes Its Work

THE Emergency Committee in Aid of Displaced Foreign Scholars was established in the conviction of the universality of scholarship, in the belief that science and learning know no national and ideological boundaries. It was founded with a great primary objective: to save the scholarship and research ability of the scholars driven out of the universities of Europe by the Nazi fury and also to serve learning and education in the United States. The fine group of American scholars and administrators who form the Committee did not found it as a relief organization for refugees generally. Fortunately relief organizations did exist and the Emergency Committee was enabled to concentrate upon its own objective. Its existence had been of necessity prolonged beyond its expectation, and that fact brought some difficult problems in its train.

It had long been the hope of the Committee, in addition to its National Research Associates program, to make some provision for its older men and women who had reached or passed the age of retirement, and who did not have savings or pensions on which to live. Unfortunately this ambition of the Committee was not realized. It has been estimated that a capital fund of several millions of dollars would have to be established were anything like a living subvention to be given those fine men and women who have devoted their whole lives to scholarship. Many of the displaced German scholars had been unjustly and illegally deprived of their pension privileges by the Nazi government. This fact has been brought to the attention of the Department of State by the Committee with the request that in the peace that is to be made with Germany, the injustice may be remedied.

Of the Committee's total list of grantees and Fellows (exclusive of National Research Associates and scholars now deceased), seventy-four had reached the age of sixty years or more by 1947. It is too much to hope that all these scholars and scientists will be able to retire on pensions when the day comes on which, according to university regulations, they must leave their active teaching life. It can be appreciated with what anxiety the displaced scholars regard the advent of that time. Few if any have independent incomes. Not all by any means have children who can care for them adequately —nor is the generosity of children always sweet to the professional person who has worked independently and been self-sustaining all his mature life.

Through its National Research Associates program, the Emergency Committee has been able to take care of a small handful. Because the Committee's activities have emphasized grants to the preeminent among the refugee scholars, it has been inevitable that the average age of the grantees has been high. And because Hitler's regime lasted twelve long years, it followed that the scholars who were in their early fifties when they first came to the United States shortly after 1933, have now reached and passed their sixtieth birthday. The foundation or groups of foundations which can work out some plan whereby these scholars who will soon reach the age of retirement can enjoy fruitful activity unmarred by worry about their next week's sustenance, will have performed a humane service and one which will at the same time confer a real benefit upon the cultural life of this country.

As the day of victory for the United Nations approached in Europe the Emergency Committee took stock of its accomplishments: It had secured places in 145 colleges and universities and institutions scattered throughout the country for 288 displaced scholars under its original program and for many of the 47 professional people under the Rosenwald Plan. By its advice and encouragement it had enabled others to find places in industrial, financial, and commercial corporations. (It has been estimated that during the year in which the Committee drew its work to a close, the earnings of its scholars alone exceeded $800,000.) With the advance of the Allied armies the persecution of scholars in Europe because of race, religion, and political opinions was stopped, and with it the exodus of scholars from Europe was much diminished. Not all who had reached our shores had been successfully placed. But the outlook was not bad. It is true that with the demobilization of the armies many college and university teachers returned to their former teaching positions, sometimes filled in their absence by displaced scholars. But it was known that some did not desire to return. Moreover at the time of the victory in Europe, June 1, 1945, more than 650,000 soldiers had indicated their intention to take advantage of the recently enacted G.I. Bill of Rights providing that any soldier might renew his interrupted college career or begin a college career if he were a high school graduate at the expense of the federal government. That number is more than half of all the students at college when the United States entered the war. As of February, 1948 it was estimated that the number of veteran students in our colleges and universities amounted to 1,300,000. With the additional generation of civilian students the prospect was that the colleges and universities would be crowded with students at the end of the war. If that outlook proved to be true, even the displaced scholars who had been recruited only temporarily to fill the places of American teachers needed for the war effort would probably be retained. Finally, experience has shown that the best of the displaced scholars had secured positions. It was not the desire of the Emergency Committee to obtain posts for mediocre scholars. The Committee was in complete agreement with the opinion expressed in the following letter:

THE ROCKEFELLER FOUNDATION
49 West 49th Street, New York 20

November 30, 1943

DEAR PROFESSOR DUGGAN:

. . . The reasons for taking this view [bringing the work of the Committee to a close] are that the main purpose for starting the Committee and for its greatest success, i.e., a large number of displaced scholars of singular importance of whose potential contributions and availability American universities were clearly unaware, has in large measure ceased to exist. The most effective and appropriate placements and adjustments have been made: The law of diminishing return has set in. The postwar influx which may come will bring another set of problems, and if it is met at all it should be divorced from the wartime refugee procedures. Philanthropic funds will be more needed for the re-creation of European universities than for the staffing of our universities with more Europeans. Judged by any means known to me we have reached the saturation point. Before long we shall have passed it, for postwar academic positions will be reserved for returning Americans to the deliberate exclusion of any others.

It is evident that for some of the Committee's stipendiaries the closing of the Committee work will represent a real hardship. I cannot foresee any time when this will not be the case even more than now. But I doubt if the Committee either ideally or practically could desirably become a permanent accessory of the American academic scene.

You have done in an unprecedented set of circumstances a service to American scholarship unparalleled in our brief history. It is the modern equivalent to the exodus of scholars to Italy after the fall of Constantinople, or the spread of French Protestants after the Revocation of the Edict of Nantes. At all events no group in America has acted more wisely in behalf of the scholars and more intelligently in behalf of the universities than your Committee, and I am consoled by the record of this ten-year-old Emergency Committee.

Yours sincerely,

ALAN GREGG

No account of the Committee's grantees would be complete without a word about the scholars who returned to Europe when their grants had expired. There were some dozen of them. Four were Frenchmen, who returned as soon as their country was liberated—one, Jacques Maritain, to serve as French Ambassador to the Holy See. One, a Norwegian, returned to his homeland after the Nazis were driven out. Another small group went back to the Old World before the outbreak of war to take up academic posts—one at Odessa, and one as Director of the Observatory in Istanbul where he later died. Others had gone back because they believed there was no clear need for them here.

It was mentioned earlier that the Emergency Committee was supported almost exclusively by the generosity of Jewish foundations and individuals. The situation of the Jewish population in the European war zones was indescribably bad. They were wandering throughout Central and Eastern Europe, homeless, starving, and often almost naked. The governments of the countries concerned had not adequate resources to give the needed relief. The Jewish citizenry of the United States would of necessity bear the major share of the burden of relief for their co-religionists in Europe. Because the members of the Emergency Committee believed their objective had been fairly well accomplished, and because they did not want in the slightest degree to be an obstacle to the great task confronting the Jewish population of the United States, the Emergency Committee formally disbanded as of June 1, 1945. They arranged to deposit their records in the archives of the New York Public Library where they would form part of the permanent collection of that institution, to be kept under lock and seal for a period of twenty-five years. In this way they sought to preserve for the use of scholars in generations to come the mass of important historical and biographical material which the Committee had collected during its years of service.

CHAPTER VI

Fields of Study and Geographical Distribution
of the Displaced Scholars

THE Committee throughout its long career acted on the principle that the universities and colleges to which it made grants should exercise full right of choice as to whom they wished to call, as well as free judgment concerning fields of study in which they believed they could introduce newcomers without overloading curricula, antagonizing faculty members or bringing foreigners into unfair competition with American teachers. Fields of study represented by scholars in whose behalf our grants were made, therefore, were determined by the action of the universities and not by any solicitation or pressure on the part of the Committee. A glance at the disciplines for which the Committee's grants were made (see Appendix I) is not without interest as showing fields in which American institutions believed they need not fear competition or in which they welcomed new blood.

It appeared to be the conviction of American educators that there was more opportunity for foreign scholars in the humanities than in any other branch of learning. Of the total of 335 stipendiaries of the Committee (including grantees, National Research Associates, and Rosenwald Fellows), 137, or about two-fifths, were representatives of the humanities. An apparent preference for men and women who had been trained as philologists or teachers of language and literature is evidenced by the fact that 43 of the people in the humanities came from those fields. Of the others: 27 were art historians or archaeologists, and 22 represented philosophy. Music and musicology together claimed 18.

The division of learning in which educators declared themselves least ready to engage displaced professors was social science. It was commonly said that for the teaching of American youth at the undergraduate level there was no substitute for the American sociologist or economist who, steeped in the scientific literature as well as the folkways of this country, knew conditions here and understood American young people. In spite of this fact, a not inconsiderable portion of the entire group of stipendiaries—110 out of 335—were men and women in the social sciences. Interestingly enough, some 33 of this number came from the field of law. A word of explanation about this category should be offered. In most continental universities there are but four traditional faculties: law, medicine, philosophy, and theology. With the growth of branches of knowledge in other fields, they became incorporated into some one of these four, e.g., history, economics, government, diplomacy, politics, and some other branches would be studied under the faculty of law. Hence when displaced scholars in these latter branches first arrived they sometimes stated in answer to inquiries as to their field of work that it was law. This explains the large number under law in the statistics. The versatility of the legal group after their arrival in this country was striking. Not a few men from Europe who had gone so far as to specialize as professors, Privatdozenten, or assistants in the law faculties of foreign universities, changed over into other fields in the United States, turning their talents with a good measure of success to philosophy, classics, history, or even in one instance to zoology. Economics also accounted for 33 scholars in the social sciences group, with history claiming 19 and sociology 14.

Comparatively speaking, there were not many natural scientists on the Committee's roster—81 out of a total of 335, or less than a quarter. Looking back over their years of activity, members of the Committee often recall their anxiety lest they bring in too many physicists and mathematicians to strive with young Americans for the few vacant posts in colleges and universities. With the outbreak of war, however, there may have been some regret that we had not invited more scientists in these fields to help supply the crying demand for scientific personnel in the war effort. It is certain that the Committee's 26 mathematicians, 16 physicists, and 7 chemists were kept particularly busy during those years—as indeed were most of the qualified scientists in the refugee group who were known to the Committee.

Because of the existence of specialized services to help refugees in the field of medicine, the medical sciences represented a field in which the Emergency Committee in Aid of Displaced Foreign Scholars properly exercised little activity. It was somewhat by exception that a few grants were made in this department to men who were active in the Hebrew University in cancer research and gynecology. Former professors or Privatdozenten from the medical faculties of foreign universities who had been deprived of their posts by the Nazis were not in principle, however, ineligible for our support; and a total of seven grants in all were given in the field of medicine.

GEOGRAPHICAL DISTRIBUTION

As was natural, the greatest single concentration of scholars and professional people on subvention from the Committee or receiving aid indirectly in the form of salary payments

from the institutions to which our grants were made, occurred in New York State. Not only did many refugees tend
of their own accord to cluster near the main port of entry
where they found friends and compatriots, but among the
displaced scholars there was a certain fear of what they would
find in the small colleges as opposed to the great urban universities. Some European professors whose academic career
had been spent at a university of international fame dreaded
loss of prestige if they entered upon American teaching life
in a rural or suburban college. In European countries education is divided into three categories: elementary, secondary,
and university. In the United States there are four divisions,
the college being interposed between the secondary school
and the university. Many Europeans failed to understand the
honorable status enjoyed by the college in the American
world of higher education. Anxiety was frequently expressed
also lest library facilities in the smaller institutions might not
prove adequate—a doubt that closer acquaintance with the
American scene often dispelled.

In addition to these considerations, institutions of higher
learning were numerous in the New York area and as experience showed tended to be hospitable to the newcomers.
Thirty-one different institutions in that area provided a working place for a total of 111 refugees on stipends from the
Committee, whether as grantees, as Rosenwald Fellows, or
as National Research Associates.

In New York City, the New School for Social Research
alone had at some time 17 of the Committee's scholars in
addition to 4 Fellows, making a total of 21. Columbia University, including Columbia College, Barnard College, and
Teachers College, accounted for 15 refugee scholars. New
York University had 13, of whom 5 were attached to the
Institute of Fine Arts.

Ten grantees and 1 Fellow of the Committee were enabled

to carry on their researches at the Institute of Social Research—
an association of scholars transplanted from Zurich and now
domiciled at Columbia University although not an integral
part of that institution.

Five scholars and 1 Fellow received assignments at the
New York Public Library. At the City Colleges within New
York City 6 grantees of the Committee received teaching
posts.

Of specialists in Jewish, Hebrew, and Yiddish studies working at special institutions in the metropolitan area under
stipends from the Committee, 8 were grantees.

A fruitful concentration of Committee scholars in the
eastern states occurred at the Institute for Advanced Study
at Princeton, New Jersey, where 11 grantees found an environment that was stimulating to scholarly production. It is perhaps interesting as an aside to note that although the *average*
age level of these men as of the year of the Committee's first
grant was just below forty years, 5 of the 11 were in
their thirties when first carried on the Committee's books.
This high valuation placed on the younger scholars of brilliant promise is noteworthy in that it occurred nowhere else
to such a marked degree. Although the Committee's general
policy reserved its grants for older scholars save in exceptional cases, relaxation of the rule was possible in such a situation where a scientific or scholarly institution of the Institute's standing vouched for the competence and scholarly
achievements of the men selected.

Massachusetts received 27 stipendiaries of the Committee,
of whom 13 were at Harvard (including National Research
Associates) and 4 at Massachusetts Institute of Technology.
Connecticut numbered 11, of whom 9 were at Yale University.

Pennsylvania welcomed 27 of the Committee's grantees,
with the largest concentration, 22, in the Philadelphia area.

The University of Pennsylvania alone listed 7 grantees and 1 Fellow of the Committee, while Swarthmore and Bryn Mawr each accommodated 5.

Nineteen grantees found teaching and research opportunities in the District of Columbia, including 5 each at the Library of Congress and the American University, and 3 at the Catholic University.

Kentucky took 6 of the Committee's grantees, distributed between the University of Louisville and the University of Kentucky, while Ohio, with its large number of colleges, took 9.

It was to be expected that Illinois, with its great universities and numerous progressive colleges, would be very hospitable to the refugee scholar; and 26 grantees and Fellows taught or carried on research there under subventions from the Emergency Committee, 9 of whom were at the University of Chicago. Among the new institutions to avail themselves of the Committee's grantees was Central Y.M.C.A. College in Chicago—now Roosevelt College—which engaged 5.

West of the Mississippi, California was the most important center to provide a working place for an appreciable number of the Committee's grantees. That state took 16 in all—8 of whom were attached to the University of California and 3 to Stanford.

The only institution not in the United States to share in the Committee's plan was the Hebrew University in Palestine. Certain of the Committee's funds could not be expended overseas for they were earmarked solely for use in the United States. Enough money was found, however, partially to subsidize at the Hebrew University one of the most important groups of men assisted by the Committee anywhere. Fifteen outstanding scholars and scientists found a secure and stimulating locus for their work at this most remarkable institution on Mount Scopus, where they carried on their researches in radiology and cancer research, in gynecology, and in the humanities.

It will be noted that sectarian and church-related institutions in different parts of the country found their way into the Committee's list along with the large private universities, the state universities, land-grant colleges, and small independent foundations. It is to the credit of all of them that they aided with marked impartiality scholars of different faiths. Catholic institutions were found harboring both Protestant and Jewish exiles, while the Protestant schools carried out their traditional role of religious tolerance. Jewish institutions, like Jewish funds, were at the service of all denominations.

In the many institutions with which the Committee's grantees and Fellows were connected, refugee scholars in addition to those aided by this Committee were taken on, sometimes with the help of other organizations but frequently on the budget of the institutions themselves. A great number of the Committee's own grantees, once launched on the stream of American academic life and moving from college to college when called, even as American professors are normally accustomed to doing, did not remain indefinitely at the institution to which our assistance was given but went on to other seats of learning.

THE ROSENWALD FELLOWSHIPS

An additional word should be said about the Rosenwald Fellowships. They were founded in 1942. The Emergency Committee decided at the very beginning of its career to confine its efforts to assisting mature scholars who had already made their mark in German universities and Gymnasien. William Rosenwald of the Rosenwald Family Association consulted the Executive Committee to ask whether the Emergency Committee would receive a grant from the Association to be used for the benefit of younger refugees. The fellowships established by means of the grant were not intended primarily for scholars and were to be awarded in most cases to men and women outside the teaching profession: to artists, musicians, architects, men of letters, and others who gave promise of creative work in their special fields. The aim of the fellowships was to enable the younger refugees, particularly those who had but recently arrived in this country and who had not yet had an opportunity to make their own way, to secure a foothold in their new environment as the beginning of a career which might lead to complete independence of any assistance.

Whereas scholars on the Committee's Grants-in-Aid program were, in accordance with the Committee's policy, attached to institutions of higher learning rather than enabled to participate in the academic life of the country on an independent basis, the writers, painters, sculptors, and other professional people who shared in the Rosenwald Fellowship program worked under another set of conditions. By the very nature of their work, the Fellows benefited by the opportunity to carry on their activities quietly at a writing table, often it is true in a small furnished room, in the seclusion of a rented studio, or in a cubicle of the public library. Although the occupation of certain ones took them into the laboratory or classroom of a scientific or academic institution, only 15 Fellows—less than a third of the group of forty-seven—were formally affiliated with an American institution during the term of the Committee's stipend.

Although the program for the Rosenwald Fellows was originally set up for the assistance of the younger group, great freedom of action and choice as to the age of Fellows selected and the amounts to be awarded to them was allowed the Committee when the plan went into operation. Out of a list of

147 applicants, 47 were chosen. They ranged in age from thirty-six to seventy years. Thirty-eight were men and 9 were women. There were 21 Germans, 15 Austrians, 3 Russians, 2 Hungarians, 2 Italians, 2 Czechs, and 1 each from Latvia and Poland.

The Fellows represented 14 different fields of work, with the largest concentration in the humanities. Applied art and art history claimed 13 of the total number of 47; letters came second with 8 Fellows. Out of 17 social scientists, 5 were economists.

There were many requests for renewals of these grants, but the Committee was obliged to restrict its assistance under this program to a one-year period. Renewals were refused to all but 4 Fellows, whose cases were of special merit. The usual stipend granted for a one-year period was $1,200.

The fellowships had good results. Despite the original objective of the fellowships, of the forty-seven holders eighteen became at least temporarily established in universities, colleges, and other research institutions. These placements occurred in the fields of history, art history, economics, literature, art, costume design, psychology, sociology, drama, law, and archaeology. Eleven of the Fellows carried on projects or research investigations dealing with Germany—such as anti-Semitism, labor movements in Germany, German youth, German education, and German history. Several of the fellows held highly successful art exhibitions in New York galleries; others published books which were well regarded by the critics.

As of May, 1945, the last date on which these figures were available, 28 of these Fellows had applied for their first citizenship papers, 5 had applied for final papers, five had become citizens.[1]

---

[1] A complete list of the holders of the fellowships and the fields in which they worked is given in Appendix VIII.

When the Emergency Committee came for the last time to attempt a statistical and interpretive study of its grantees, Fellows and National Research Associates, it had to face the fact that its very philosophy and chosen manner of operation had limited the quality as well as the character of available data. It had at no time sought intimate or confidential information from its clients, hence its files were lacking in such material about them. (It should be added that the scholars were by and large a group of composed, objective personalities little given even under extreme stress to pouring out their frustrations or heartaches in the course of interviews or in letters or reports from the field.) The Committee had been meticulous in avoiding interference in relationships between the refugee professor and the institution which wished his services. Much of the story of these relationships, therefore, was not directly known to the Committee. Moreover, it had respected the scholars' almost unanimous desire to shun publicity and their disinclination to answer forms and questionnaires, and had made a very restricted use of such research instruments in its dealings with them. Frequently the extent of the Committee's knowledge about its early grantees beyond certain vital statistics was that celebrated scholarly and scientific people judged their work to be of outstanding importance, and that leading American institutions asked for the privilege of adding them to their faculties.

It should not be thought that in the first years of the Committee's work all scholars who were to benefit from grants came into the Committee's office on their way to the university to which they had been called. Certain scholars were never interviewed by members of the staff at any time in their career. As time went on, however, with more publicity inevitably attending our work through the achievements of eminent grantees, and as refugee scholars began to attend annual conferences of scientists and educators meeting and talking with other scholars about their common interests, and as the Committee's own policy with regard to placement changed from a passive to an active one, face-to-face contact with new grantees became essential. By the time the Committee's Fellowship program had gotten under way in 1942, an interview with each candidate was mandatory, and detailed biographical material was required.

In a review of the marital status of its 288 grantees and National Research Associates, 209 were found to be married and 31 single. Three had been widowed and 2 divorced, while concerning 43 the Committee had incomplete information. Somewhat less than a dozen of the scholars had married American women. At least 131 had one child or more.

The preponderant number of the Committee's grantees were male. Of the total group of 288 grantees and National Research Associates, only 13, or less than 5 per cent, were women. In this small but distinguished group, 3 had been professors in German universities and 2 Privatdozenten, while the others had been variously active as curators, librarians, researchers, and social workers.

Of the Committee's 47 Rosenwald Fellows, 25 were married, 13 single, 4 widowed, and 1 was divorced. Information was lacking about 4. Eleven of the group were parents.

CHAPTER VII

Cooperation of the Emergency Committee with Other Organizations

THOUGH the Emergency Committee in all probability assisted more of the displaced scholars than any other organization, it was by no means the only organization devoted to their service. Some organizations already in existence turned their attention to the problem as soon as it arose. Others, especially of a professional nature, were organized for the specific purpose of assisting in the placement of refugees in the particular profession. Practically all the organizations cooperated most heartily in the work of the Emergency Committee.

THE ROCKEFELLER FOUNDATION

Even before the organization of the Emergency Committee, the Rockefeller Foundation had undertaken its extensive program in aid of the displaced scholars. From the very beginning of the Emergency Committee's activities Dr. Alan Gregg, Director of the Medical Sciences of the Rockefeller Foundation and Thomas B. Appleget, the Foundation's Vice President, sat in at executive committee meetings of the Emergency Committee and rendered great service with their advice, the result of the long and continuous experience of the Rockefeller Foundation in the field of international scholarship and scientific collaboration. The contribution of the Rockefeller Foundation, however, was not confined to advice. From the beginning of the activities of the Emergency Committee, it duplicated in almost all cases the grant made by the Emergency Committee to a college or university receiving a displaced scholar. With the passage of time, when the grants made by the Emergency Committee had to be reduced because of the increased demands upon its resources the Rockefeller Foundation continued its original contributions. By the close of 1945, when its refugee scholar program ended, the Foundation had expended $1,410,778 for the purpose and had aided 303 individual scholars.

In the face of the new emergency caused by the sudden undeclared war by Germany upon the countries of Western Europe, the Rockefeller Foundation generously came forward to give additional assistance to the cause of the displaced scholars. Dr. Alvin Johnson, Director of the New School for Social Research, had already organized the University in Exile for the benefit of displaced German scholars and now offered to receive refugee scholars from other countries and to find chairs for them in the University in Exile provided funds were forthcoming. Such definite appointments were necessary in order to meet the requirements laid down in the immigration law that a foreigner may not be admitted to the United States unless a guarantee is given that he will not become a public charge. Our consuls abroad also regarded closely the provision of the Immigration Act which required that the scholar entering on a professor's visa must have taught the last two years before leaving Europe and must have received an invitation to teach in an American college or university.

To enable the New School to carry out its part of the plan, the Executive Committee appropriated $35,000 to the School for additional operating expenses over a two-year period. Subsequent appropriations raised the total granted for this purpose to $65,589. By 1940 the Emergency Committee had become highly regarded in practically all our institutions of higher education for its work with refugee scholars, and it at once put all its facilities at the service of the new group of displaced scholars. The Rockefeller Foundation made a grant to the Emergency Committee of $10,000 a year for two years to enable it to assist in the administration of the additional activity involved in the organization of a placement program. Under the plan, the New School, the Institute of International Education, and the Emergency Committee were authorized to recommend scholars to the Foundation. Final decision in all cases, however, rested with the Foundation. The Foundation also nominated scholars directly. Actually, over 60% of the initial grants were made to the New School. The grant covered travel expense and stipend, ranging from $1,500 to $2,500 annually for two years. Under its Emergency Program the Foundation expended a total of $348,794 in grants for fifty-two individual scholars. The Emergency Committee wishes to record its tribute to the Rockefeller Foundation for the splendid service it rendered to the cause of learning and scholarship by its prolonged assistance to the refugee scholars.

THE UNIVERSITY IN EXILE

Because of the important work of the New School for Social Research in connection with refugee scholars, Dr. Alvin Johnson, its Director, was asked to contribute a statement which follows:

In the spring of 1933, when the first list of German university professors expelled from their chairs was published, the New School for Social Research launched a project for assembling a group of these professors to form a well coordinated Faculty of the Political and Social Sciences.

The Director of the New School had for many years been impressed by the international character of scholarship, and had been an adherent of the aims and ideals of Dr. Stephen Duggan's Institute of International Education. With most of the scholars dismissed by Hitler the Director of the School had been in correspondence, and some of them had contributed articles of great value to the *Encyclopaedia of the Social Sciences* of which he was Editor. It was clear that the Nazi policy, in destroying academic freedom in Germany, had in effect exiled the German university as the world knew it. Hence the name adopted for the proposed Faculty by the New School: the University in Exile.

At the same time Dr. Duggan was working out a far more extensive project involving the placement of exiled professors in all the leading educational institutions of the country. At an early interview between Dr. Duggan and the Director of the New School it was recognized that the two plans were in complete harmony. The Emergency Committee plan offered opportunity to a wide range of American scholars and students to benefit from the abilities of excellent German professors. The New School plan offered the possibility of an organized group, carrying on cooperatively the methods by which German political and social science had latterly won eminence. The Emergency Committee plan looked to the assimilation into America of the individual scholar. The New School looked to the assimilation of a Faculty as a whole. It was agreed that both plans held out significant promise for American scholarship. And as additional lists of proscribed professors were published from week to week, it became ever clearer that there was room for two plans, indeed for many plans.

Certain specific differences were obvious from the start. Under the plan of the Emergency Committee, the initiative in employing professors lay with the universities and colleges. The New School, as an operating institution, could issue its invitations, carrying non-quota visas, without any delay. The difference was not important, at first, owing to the extraordinary efficiency of the Emergency Committee in animating the universities and colleges. It became important when the French army collapsed, placing scores of refugee professors in France in instant jeopardy, a situation that will be discussed later.

In this first interview between Dr. Duggan and the Director of the New School it was agreed that the New School would seek independent sources of support. This it succeeded promptly in doing, thanks to the magnificent generosity of Hiram J. Halle, who underwrote its requirement of $60,000 a year for two years. The New School undertook two other limitations on its own action. It resolved that members of its own Faculty would not be candidates for positions that could be filled by candidates of the Emergency Committee. This did not preclude the acceptance of non-subsidized positions, and a number of the men brought over by the New School have accepted such positions. The New School also resolved that it would not appeal to the Emergency Committee for grants. But with the steady increase of European scholars who needed to be taken care of the New School had to drop this limitation. Some twenty-one grants were made to the New School by the Emergency Committee, many of them at the generous suggestion of Dr. Duggan.

It is too early to appraise the effectiveness of the New School plan for American scholarship. If the publication of books and articles in scientific magazines is taken as a criterion, the New School plan of an organic Faculty has worked well. If its appeal to students is a criterion, it has also worked well. The University in Exile, now known as the Graduate Faculty, has more students than most university faculties in America. No student of American education can doubt that the Emergency Committee plan has worked well. There are scores of American institutions whose intellectual life has been greatly enriched by the distinguished scholars introduced by the Emergency Committee.

The educational consequences of the fall of France created a new justification for the New School plan, if any were needed. All refugee, liberal, and Jewish professors in France were at the mercy of the Nazi conquerors, who had passed on from expulsion and confiscation to torture and murder. It was no longer possible to wait for action by university presidents and faculties, as in the early days of the Emergency Committee. Instant action was required. The Director of the New School petitioned the Rockefeller Foundation for grants to cover transportation expenses and two year stipends for, at the outside, a hundred scholars, officially invited to the Faculties of the New School, but placeable in any institution better equipped to use their services. The petition was granted, and the cables were kept hot with messages of invitation to scholars who had already lost hope. Similar appeals to the Carnegie Corporation and the Belgian American Educational Foundation met a ready response. So also appeals to private individuals. By the gallant support of the American consuls something over a hundred scholars were rescued from the teeth of the Nazi hyena.

Most of these scholars were distributed through the universities—some of them to play a material part in the construction of the atomic bomb. A contingent of the social sciences and the liberal arts remained with the New School, to form the Ecole Libre des Hautes Etudes, for a time the only freely functioning French university. It is functioning still*, and has high hopes of permanence, as a liaison between French and American university life, an outpost in the system of international education, of which Dr. Stephen Duggan is the great leader, and the New School for Social Research an ardent follower.

THE IRANIAN INSTITUTE AND SCHOOL FOR ASIATIC STUDIES

From Dr. Arthur Upham Pope, Director of the Iranian Institute, comes this account of the building of a curriculum of Asiatic studies around a core of refugee scholars:

One of the earliest grants of the Emergency Committee was to the Iranian Institute for the salary of Dr. Richard Ettinghausen. That the grant was justified is indicated by the fact that Dr. Ettinghausen subsequently became Professor of Islamic Art in the University of Michigan, Editor of *Ars Islamica,* and is now Curator of Near Eastern Art in the Freer Gallery.

More important grants came again at a critical time when the Nazi Anschluss in Austria released several important men from the University of Vienna. Through the assistance of the Emergency Committee it was possible to add to our staff Pro-

---

* The Ecole Libre des Hautes Etudes became an independent institution in 1947.

fessor Bernhard Geiger, thought by many to be the outstanding scholar in the field of Indo-Iranian language and literature. At the same time Professor Gustave von Grünebaum, a brilliant Arabist, was added; he was subsequently called to the University of Chicago.

Grants from the Emergency Committee made possible the further addition to the faculty of Dr. Leo Oppenheim, a brilliant scholar in the field of early Mesopotamian studies. Dr. William Haas, a noted historian of Oriental civilization, and Professor von Heine-Geldern were aided by grants at critical times which enabled us to retain them on our staff.

These grants made possible the nucleus of a School of Asiatic Studies. We are pleased to report that the appointments were of the finest character, that the spirit of cooperation and good will, and the adjustment to the flexibility needed for a pioneer enterprise were all and more than could be expected. I doubt that any grants that the Emergency Committee made could have had a greater significance than those given to our Institute; and the Institute is gratefully aware that these grants required courage and imagination, which we believe have been justified by the results. The School of Asiatic Studies, which was not in existence when the first grant was made, has made as high as 165 registrations. The faculty has grown from nothing to a resident full-time faculty of 14. The resources of the Institute, chiefly in the form of unusual *objets d'art,* have increased from approximately $10,000 to a value well in excess of $600,000. During this period the intellectual productivity of the Institute has been extraordinary. It seems improbable that any comparable group has made so many important contributions in so short a time. If this desirable end is achieved, the faith and generosity of the Emergency Committee will have been an indispensable factor.

THE INSTITUTE OF FINE ARTS OF NEW YORK UNIVERSITY

Dr. Walter W. S. Cook, the Director of the Institute, writes as follows:

The rise of the Hitler regime and the domination of Germany by the Nazi party brought about a real Renaissance in the study of the Fine Arts in this country. At the time of the German election in April, 1933, Dr. Erwin Panofsky was here as a Visiting Professor from the University of Hamburg which, as in 1931 and 1932, had given him a leave of absence to our Institute of Fine Arts of New York University. At once he was added to our staff as a permanent professor. After teaching for two years on our staff, he accepted a new position at the Institute for Advanced Study at Princeton, New Jersey. He has, however, constantly maintained a personal connection with our Institute where, as Lecturer, he has given each year one or two courses for our students. Altogether the Institute of Fine Arts of New York University was assisted by the Emergency Committee in aiding five displaced scholars to its staff.

The history of art and archaeology is a relatively recent field of study in this country, and there were relatively few Americans sufficiently equipped to teach graduate students in this field. But as a result of the addition of so many able scholars from Europe, numerous American students have been, and are now, receiving a training rarely received in this country before. The great contribution made at our Institute of Fine Arts is that these scholars have trained, and are still training, a new generation of American students, who will in turn be capable of instructing future generations of American students. At present, students come here from all parts of this country as well as from Central and South America, and Canada for advanced graduate instruction for the degrees of M.A. and Ph.D. Thus the instruction given our students by these foreign scholars has proved to be a very effective force in the progress of American scholarship in the history of art and archaeology. For this consummation we owe much to the generosity of the Emergency Committee.

THE NATIONAL RESEARCH ASSOCIATES

In the early part of 1939 Professor Harlow Shapley of Harvard University established the Harvard National Research Associates. These consisted of a small group of displaced scholars of an age beyond that at which places might be readily found in a college or university. The facilities of the library and laboratories of Harvard were to be placed at their disposal for personal research, but they were not required to give instruction. Moneys which had been raised by the efforts of Professor Shapley were subsequently, by arrangement with the donors and with the full consent of Harvard University, turned over to the Emergency Committee in Aid of Displaced Foreign Scholars in trust to carry out the purposes for which this fund was collected. Five of the original group at Harvard University were taken over by the Emergency Committee, and six other distinguished scholars, fifty-eight years of age or older, were added from among the Emergency Committee's own grantees at other institutions. Of these men two, who could not be added to the regular list, were added to the grantees of the National Research Associates for one year by virtue of a special arrangement. As in the case of Harvard, the universities agreed that the Associates should be enabled to carry on the same type of scholarly pursuit as members of their permanent professorial staff. In almost all cases the National Research Associates remained dependent on the particular funds in this account. This did not mean life tenure for any scholars, but rather that a modest yearly grant would be available to them so long as the principal and interest of the Fund should last.

THE OBERLAENDER TRUST

Another organization which was in continuous cooperation with the Emergency Committee was the Oberlaender Trust of Philadelphia, of which Dr. Wilbur K. Thomas was Secretary.

The Oberlaender Trust was an offshoot of the Carl Schurz Memorial Foundation, which had been organized in 1930 and was supported by funds contributed by American citizens chiefly of German descent. The Trust had been established in 1931 by Gustav Oberlaender with an endowment of one million dollars. The Carl Schurz Memorial Foundation had been organized to develop cultural relations with Germany and to stimulate an interest in the contributions made to American civilization by Germans, as in the case of the so-called "Pennsylvania Dutch." The Oberlaender Trust had the same objectives as the Carl Schurz Memorial Foundation, but its regulations permitted it to use its funds for assistance to refugees.

The methods of the Oberlaender Trust differed from those of the Emergency Committee in some respects, though the objective was the same. The Oberlaender Trust concerned itself with all kinds of refugees from Germany: scholars, physicians, lawyers, technicians, musicians, and others. Contrary to the practice followed by the Emergency Committee, the Trust dealt directly with the refugees. It had no objection to the practice whereby the scholar himself sought a place in a college or university on his own initiative. In cases where the scholar was successful, the Trust would consider making a grant to the institution as part of his salary. In fact, the Trust was willing to assist a refugee who had secured a teaching position even though he might not have taught before. The Trust did not require of an institution a definite promise of permanent employment, but rather the assurance that there was an actual opening in the man's field. The Trust followed the practice of making small grants to refugees, even as small as $100 if this would assist a refugee to get a start. Sometimes these small grants were in the form of loans. Like the Emergency Committee the Trust believed in enabling a refugee to switch from his own field of work to some other which offered greater opportunities of employment.

As of June 28, 1945, the Oberlaender Trust had contributed over $300,000 for aid to refugees. Part of this amount had been expended to help those who were, technically speaking, displaced scholars; another part had been used to assist professionals and other refugees.

The cooperation of the Oberlaender Trust was particularly valuable in the later career of the Emergency Committee when the Trust frequently added to the reduced grant that the Emergency Committee was compelled to make, a sufficient amount to justify a college or university in extending an invitation to a displaced scholar.

ADDITIONAL COOPERATING AGENCIES

As news of the Emergency Committee's activities became generally known, requests came from institutions outside the United States for grants to enable them to invite displaced scholars to their faculties. In an attempt to rescue deposed professors from their desperate situations within their native lands, friends and interested societies sought to secure calls for them to universities in parts of Europe not yet violated and in the New World. Although the Committee had on several previous occasions seriously considered applications for stipends to be awarded Canadian and English institutions, as well as to Continental universities, it was obliged to establish as one of its prime points of policy the regulation that it could not make grants to institutions outside the United States. The one exception to this rule was that grants might be, and were, made to the Hebrew University in Palestine, where a total of fifteen displaced foreign scholars from Germany and Italy were ultimately assisted under a subvention from this Committee.

The Carnegie Corporation, during the period 1934–1940, made grants totaling $110,000 under which colleges and universities, chiefly in the British Dominions and Colonies, were enabled to arrange places on their faculties for about twenty displaced foreign scholars. Grants were sufficient to help the institutions, during an initial two-year period, to pay salaries of the scholars selected, the universities thereafter

assuming responsibility for salaries if the scholars remained
on the staffs. A few other grants were made by the Corporation to aid displaced scholars in research and publication, or
in study preparatory to teaching in a field other than that in
which they had originally specialized. Since 1940 no grants
for purposes such as the above have been made by the Corporation.

The American Friends Service Committee, though not
founded specifically to aid refugee scholars, undertook to
participate in assisting them as part of its over-all work. As
has already been made evident, many displaced scholars were
not prepared to move directly from a European post and
from refugee difficulties into university positions in the
United States. They needed preparation and orientation.
The American Friends undertook to prepare scholars and
their wives for happy and continuing relations with American
colleges. Anything that could be done to keep scholars from
living and brooding among members of their own language
groups was a forward step in orientation.

Our field secretary wrote as of October 1, 1941:

In the summer of 1940 the American Friends conducted their
first American Seminar at Wolfeboro, New Hampshire. In the
following year at the Plymouth Seminar they gathered some eighty
displaced scholars and their wives with fifty Americans. They
set up a cooperative community on the pleasant campus of the
Holderness School (Episcopal) with each member helping in
the work of the dining-room and kitchen. This was, of course, a
bit strange to some of our displaced foreign scholars, but they all
rallied round it. For two hours each morning they joined in a
lecture-discussion session, directed by Dr. Herbert Adolphus
Miller and dealing with "American sociology." There were also
group and individual lessons in English. In the evenings there
were recreation, lectures, etc. A fine relationship with the town of
Plymouth was established, with visits to the Rotary Club, the
League of Women Voters, *et al.* A concert was organized for the
benefit of the local hospital at which the talent came from the

Seminar musicians. I went up to see the experiment and some of our own displaced scholars participating in it. So many people wished personal conference that I remained for five days, while my wife and daughter joined the group of English tutors.

It was not only under the auspices of the Friends that these splendid gatherings took place, gatherings so characteristic of the American way of realizing objectives by means of the cooperative efforts of individuals and so illuminating to foreigners. They sprang up in widely scattered parts of the country wherever refugee scholars were to be found.

On August 21, 1941, the late Ernie Pyle wrote from Stillwater, Minnesota, of "The Experiment in International Living" there:

This is its second year. It has about ten foreign professors, ten visiting students from the East, and more than a hundred local students, most of them Stillwater adults. . . . The professors get no pay. But each one is housed free by a local family; in return the whole family can go to school for nothing. The professors make some extra money by giving private lessons and putting on plays and operettas. . . . Classes are held both day and night. Stillwater people can attend the entire summer for $12. a family. They can study French, Spanish, Italian, or German. They can study stagecraft, music appreciation, dramatics, or history. They can listen to lectures on "Development of Democratic Thought" or "The Nations of Europe," etc.

The Committee adhered to its decision to secure positions for scholars alone in spite of the increasing demand for places by physicians, lawyers, and civil servants driven from their homes in Germany. Our trustee, Dr. Alfred E. Cohn, was requested by the Committee to investigate among American physicians the possibility of organizing an Emergency Committee for Displaced German Physicians. In this effort which he undertook with energy and enthusiasm he was completely successful, and on November 18, 1933, the Physicians' Committee was organized with Dr. Bernard Sachs as Chairman, Dr. George Baehr as Secretary, and Dr. Edwin Beer as Treasurer. Refugees in the field of medicine gained immeasurably from the assistance of this committee of specialists. Pressure upon the Scholars Committee was relieved at the same time. It proved much more difficult to render assistance to lawyers. Refugee German lawyers were usually unfamiliar with our system of law and the administration of our courts. A very few distinguished scholars in jurisprudence were awarded positions in some of our important law schools to give courses on the philosophy of law. A considerable number of lawyers wisely undertook to follow retraining courses in other fields of work, with good results.

Among the organizations with which the Emergency Committee cooperated, one of the most effective of the small committees to serve refugees from the professional fields was the Committee for the Re-education of Refugee Lawyers, which grew out of the efforts of the Committee for the Guidance of Professional Personnel. The Committee for the Re-education of Refugee Lawyers, product of joint efforts of the law schools and the American Bar in raising money and exploring possibilities, granted nine fellowships for the academic year 1939–1940, and nineteen additional ones for the year 1940–1941. Thus a total of twenty-eight men were enabled to undergo retraining courses in the law at twenty-one different colleges and universities, scattered over a sufficiently wide area to be fairly representative of the whole United States.

The initial sums raised, as well as the initial impetus, were the product of the generosity of the New York Bar, acting under the leadership of John W. Davis, the Committee's Chairman; Arthur A. Ballantine, its Treasurer; and Walter Mendelsohn, its Secretary. Professor David Riesman of the University of Buffalo served as secretary of a selection committee of university professors, whose task it was to select men for retraining and to make arrangements for their studies in law schools throughout the country.

Since the Committee for the Re-education of Refugee Lawyers wished to spread its limited funds as far as possible, and to elicit cooperation in the communities to which the fellowship recipients went, it established the policy that it would meet no more than half the living expenses of the Fellow; his tuition and the balance of his living expenses would ordinarily have to be provided locally. Since, moreover, the schools were required to relax their academic requirements, and to institute special speed-up courses for the men, it was at first believed that not many schools would be able to afford cooperation. When, however, after the initial success of the program in 1939 and 1940, a number of additional schools, and the communities in which they were situated, volunteered to help, it became imperative for the Committee to raise additional funds, in order to match with its own commitments the commitments made by local groups throughout the country. Mr. Davis and his associates generously renewed their appeal to the donors who had originally contributed, and in almost every case they pledged additional amounts. The National Refugee Service, Inc. made a contribution, and Samuel S. Fels, the noted Philadelphia philanthropist, assured the success of the Committee's work at a critical point by guaranteeing to match local contributions up to $5,000— the limit which was, in fact, reached.

The following law schools cooperated: the University of Buffalo, University of California, University of Chicago, Columbia University, University of Pennsylvania, Tulane University, Southern Methodist University, University of Wisconsin, State University of Iowa, University of Colorado, University of Cincinnati, University of Toledo, Harvard University, Washington University in St. Louis, John B. Stetson

University, Western Reserve University, Yale University, New York University, Fordham University, Ohio State University, and The College of William and Mary.

There had been evident for a long time an urgent need for a single organization which would serve as the center for exchange of information and advice upon the whole problem of the displaced foreign scholar. Upon the advice of the Rockefeller Foundation, the Emergency Committee was selected for that function. Following the summer of 1940, the Executive Committee of the Emergency Committee invited the following persons to join it as representatives of their organizations:

Dr. Frank Aydelotte of the Institute for Advanced Study
Dr. Hertha Kraus of the American Friends Service Committee
Dr. Alvin Johnson of the University in Exile
Dr. Henry Allen Moe of the Oberlaender Trust
Mr. Charles A. Riegelman of the National Refugee Service
Dr. Harlow Shapley of the National Research Associates

This action had the happy result of eliminating duplication of work by the various organizations concerned and of obtaining the benefit of the advice of additional experienced administrators. By means of the grant made to the Emergency Committee by the Rockefeller Foundation, the Committee was able to engage Dr. Laurens H. Seelye, former President of St. Lawrence University, as field secretary to visit colleges and universities in various parts of the United States in order to stimulate interest in the program of the Emergency Committee. At the same time an Advisory Committee was organized, composed of scholars in the different fields of learning who were eminently qualified to give the best available advice on ways and means of using the scholars to advantage. In practice, however, the cooperation of the Emergency Committee with the administrative officials of our

colleges and universities was so intimate that it was found
unnecessary to burden the members of the Advisory Committee with frequent calls for assistance. A list follows of the
members of this panel to whom the Committee's gratitude
goes out:

Ross G. Harrison
National Research Council

A. J. Olson
Association of Governing Boards
of State Universities and Allied
Institutions

William M. Hepburn
American Association of University
Professors

J. Salwyn Schapiro
American Historical Association

Ralph E. Himstead
American Association of University
Professors

Guy E. Snavely
Association of American Colleges

Waldo G. Leland
American Council of Learned Societies

Harold C. Urey
American Philosophical Society

H. M. Lydenberg
American Library Association

Malcolm M. Willey
Social Science Research Council

In the early days of the Emergency Committee the majority
of the displaced scholars assisted were Jews because the Nazi
terror was directed especially against Jews. One of the finest
attributes of the work of the Emergency Committee was that,
although its income came almost exclusively from Jewish
sources, it never made any distinction between Jewish and
non-Jewish scholars in its grants. In fact, it was only by chance
that the Committee discovered the religion of any of its
grantees since it scrupulously refrained from asking them
about their creed. A college or university had only to request
a grant for a displaced scholar of whatever race or religion
to receive immediate consideration to the extent permitted
by the resources of the Committee.

The needs of Jewish relief cases—for subsistence, employment, and resettlement—were taken care of by the National Coordinating Committee (later the National Refugee Service, Inc., which in 1946 became the United Service for New Americans, Inc.). This organization was established by the American Jewish Joint Distribution Committee as a central agency to deal with the many problems involved in the immigration and settlement of refugees in this country.

As the years passed, a Christian committee (the American Christian Committee for Refugees) made up primarily of Protestants, and a Catholic organization (the Catholic Committee for Refugees), were established to aid displaced scholars and other refugees. The Emergency Committee cooperated with these committees chiefly in the exchange of information and advice but continued to make grants to displaced scholars of all faiths. The Committee found itself leaning more and more heavily upon the Family Service Section of National Refugee Service as its work developed. Whereas originally the Committee had looked to the college or university which had invited a given professor to its faculty to charge itself with his welfare and, as his host, assist tactfully in the details of his social adjustment, the Committee was gradually brought closer to problems in the daily lives of its Fellows which were often not purely economic, and not purely physical or medical, but emotional and psychological. In all these cases the Emergency Committee was glad to be able to avail itself of friendly services of professional casework agencies.

Midway in its career the Emergency Committee suffered a grievous loss in the death of its Chairman, Dr. Livingston Farrand. Before Dr. Farrand retired as President of Cornell University on June 21, 1937, he rendered invaluable service in providing wise counsel on the policies of the Emergency Committee. During his frequent absences at Cornell, Dr. Duggan acted as temporary chairman; but after mid summer of 1937 Dr. Farrand was able to devote himself unstintedly to the work of the Committee. Unfortunately he died two and a half years later. Dr. Duggan was elected Chairman to succeed him. On this occasion the Emergency Committee adopted the following resolution presented by the Chairman:

In the death of Livingston Farrand scholarship sustains a great loss. Humanity suffers a greater loss. His life was one long devotion to noble causes. He fought the white plague and saw it conquered. He headed the Red Cross and made it a living force. He became a university president and his students lived nobler lives. His voice and his pen were ever given to causes that aimed at the freedom of the human spirit.

It was most natural that when the Emergency Committee in Aid of Displaced Foreign Scholars was formed, the Committee should have turned to Dr. Farrand for guidance. He responded with a warm affirmative. He became its Chairman and directed its work with the sympathy and wisdom needed in confronting a difficult situation replete with human cruelty.

The Emergency Committee in Aid of Displaced Foreign Scholars wishes to record its admiration and appreciation for the leadership of Dr. Farrand and its affection for him as a humane person.

(Signed)   STEPHEN DUGGAN, *Chairman*
ALFRED E. COHN
L. C. DUNN
BERNARD FLEXNER
CHARLES J. LIEBMAN
NELSON P. MEAD
FRED M. STEIN

CHAPTER VIII

Proposed Plan of the Association of American Universities for Displaced Scholars in the United States

BY 1939 the increased brutality with which the Jewish citizens of Germany were treated resulted in even more urgent appeals from persecuted scholars in Germany to organizations in other countries founded to assist them. Moreover, the presidents of American colleges and universities found their desks flooded with letters from individual refugee scholars asking for positions on their faculties. Their duties were interrupted by frequent visits from such refugees, especially younger men, who were seeking places on their own initiative. This caused some resentment on the part of college administrators. The situation had become serious when on December 31, 1938, a meeting of a number of presidents of universities was held under the auspices of the Association of American Universities at the University Club in New York City to discuss the problem of the refugee scholar. President Isaiah Bowman was unable to attend because of a meeting of his own Board of Trustees, and he requested Dr. Duggan to represent him.

Dr. Robert A. Millikan, Chairman of the Executive Council of the California Institute of Technology, who was President of the Association for that year, presided. He opened the meeting by asking Dr. Duggan to give it the benefit of the experience of the Emergency Committee. Dr. Duggan briefly described the activities of the Emergency Committee up to that time and the results accomplished, and answered many questions about the Committee's work. At the close of the discussion, President Conant of Harvard University presented a plan which he had prepared for the meeting.

This plan was largely aimed to accomplish what the Emergency Committee and the Rockefeller Foundation were already doing, but President Conant expressed the belief that greater permanency for the scholars assisted would result from securing an endowment than from continuing to rely upon the annual contributions upon which the current method relied. He also insisted upon the need for more adequate support and what he considered a less hit-and-miss method of selecting the individuals to be assisted.

His plan required that a committee be appointed to have charge of selecting the men to be given assistance. He heartily approved of the Emergency Committee's suggestion of a small stipend for the older scholars and the exclusion of the younger men. This last he believed could be secured by placing the qualifications so high that only those who had "arrived" would be within the group which would be under the committee's control. Upon being asked his opinion on that point, Dr. Duggan expressed his belief that each university knew best the kind of man and in most cases the individual man most suited to its needs.

President Conant's second point was that the universities should be relieved of the burden of the support of the refugee. Instead of the present method of helping the university whereby the Emergency Committee and the Rockefeller Foundation paid the salary of a refugee for one or possibly two years with the understanding that he would then be absorbed and his salary paid by the university, there should be established a large fund from the interest on which the salary of the refugee would be paid. The salary would be fixed at $2,000, and the refugees would not be on the university ladder obstructing the advance upward of American teachers. President Conant stated that he considered $6,000,000 as the minimum sum required. That was the general opinion of those present, if President Conant's plan was adopted. The important question was where the money was to come from. Dr. Butler, President of Columbia University, thought that, as most of the refugee scholars were Jews, the necessary money might be raised from wealthy Jews. President Conant asked Dr. Duggan's opinion upon that suggestion, and Dr. Duggan stated that he did not believe the amount could be obtained in the light of the immense demands already being made upon the Jewish community. Moreover, when requested to give his opinion as to the probability of a favorable result following an appeal to the Rockefeller Foundation, Dr. Duggan stated that he thought the answer would be negative because the Rockefeller Foundation believed that the present plan was bringing about good results.

As a result of much discussion it was considered wise to appeal to well-to-do Jewish citizens and the foundations. Presidents Conant, Butler, and Dodds were appointed a Committee to revise the program presented by President Conant and to secure the signatures of the officers of the Association of American Universities, the Association of State Universities, the Association of Urban Universities, the Association of American Colleges, and the signatures of individual presidents whose names would be influential. The Committee was to visit the foundations and attempt to secure the cooperation of wealthy Jews.

On January 28, 1939, the requested report was accepted. It was entitled, "Proposed Program for Joint Action by the

American Universities to Provide an Asylum for Those Refugees from European Countries Who Are Distinguished Members of the International Community of Scholars— Declaration of Principles." The text of the report follows:

1. The American universities and colleges recognize the gravity of the present situation and the unique character of the problems presented by the expulsion of many eminent professors from their chairs in a number of countries. The American universities and colleges further recognize the importance of taking some joint action to assist the members of the academic world who are today suffering through no fault of their own and who have been deprived of their opportunity of contributing to the advancement of knowledge. This action is to be undertaken as part of the responsibility of all universities throughout the world to protect the solidarity of the international company of scholars and to further that ancient university tradition which recognized no racial or national barriers to free inquiry or the promotion of sound learning.

2. It is the belief of the undersigned administrative heads of the American universities and colleges that in making appointments to the staff merit alone should be considered. In filling both teaching and research positions the aim should always be to obtain the services of the person best qualified irrespective of race or national affiliation. Always bearing in mind the importance of developing the young talent of the country, it is desirable to give preference to citizens of this country if two men of equal merit are available, one of whom is from a foreign land.

3. It follows from the above paragraph that it is highly undesirable to place refugee professors on the staffs of American universities and colleges except on the basis of merit alone as determined by comparison with scholars throughout the world. A refugee scholar so placed should receive a salary comparable to salaries paid by the university to other men of similar distinction. However, to assist in the present emergency and to carry out their responsibilities under section one, the American universities and colleges agree to provide a sanctuary for as many refugee members of the academic community as can be accommodated. To this end it is proposed that there be established with the aid of funds to be raised from new sources, a number of

asylum fellowships with a stipend of $1,500 to $2,500 annually to be awarded by a joint committee of the American universities and colleges. It is hoped that these fellowships may be financed on an annuity basis, thus providing for the minimum living expenses of the holder without responsibility for his future on the part of the university or college in which he resides. It is proposed that the joint committee shall explore the possibility of providing hospitality for these refugee fellows at universities and colleges, or at libraries and laboratories maintained by other agencies. Such hospitality would include facilities for a continuation of the refugee's scholarly or scientific work but would not involve any teaching or administrative services from the fellows. It would be expected that the holders of these special refugee fellowships would devote themselves to a continuation of their scholarly or scientific work and would thus strengthen the life of the community of scholars with which they were associated without in any way interfering with the future of the young men on the staff and without prejudice to the filling of positions on the basis of merit alone.

> HENRY MERRITT WRISTON, Brown University
> ROBERT A. MILLIKAN, California Institute of Technology
> NICHOLAS MURRAY BUTLER, Columbia University
> EDMUND E. DAY, Cornell University
> JAMES B. CONANT, Harvard University
> ISAIAH BOWMAN, Johns Hopkins University
> ALEXANDER G. RUTHVEN, University of Michigan
> FRANK P. GRAHAM, University of North Carolina
> THOMAS S. GATES, University of Pennsylvania
> HAROLD W. DODDS, Princeton University
> JOHN L. NEWCOMB, University of Virginia
> CHARLES SEYMOUR, Yale University

No finer statement of the true position of the scholar in the university community has yet been made. Unfortunately the growing tension between Germany and its neighbors diverted attention from cultural problems, and before there was adequate time to implement the Plan the war between Germany, France, and Great Britain broke out. This brought about a new and more serious situation which required a different kind of treatment. The great Foundations turned their attention to the problems of relief, and the Jews, rich and poor, to organizing for the mere survival of their co-religionists as a people. In the meantime, the Emergency Committee continued to carry on by the methods which had proved reasonably adequate up to that time.

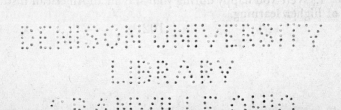

CHAPTER IX

The Displaced Scholars Speak for Themselves

UP TO the present chapter the authors have devoted themselves to describing the advent of the displaced scholars in our country and their manifold and different experiences in our institutions of higher education. We believe, however, that the reader would like to learn what conclusions the scholars themselves have drawn from their experiences, especially the evaluation they made of the standards of higher education in the United States. It was to that end that the appended letter was addressed to each of our grantees.

November 9, 1945

DEAR ————:

We are engaged in writing the history of the Emergency Committee in Aid of Displaced Foreign Scholars, which as you know came into existence following Hitler's accession to power, and which, after twelve years of activity during which it made a number of grants to American colleges and universities in behalf of displaced professors and teachers, terminated its work on June 1, 1945.

We are anxious to have your reaction to the situation which you met while a member of the staff of an American institution of higher learning, and I am wondering whether you would be willing to answer the following questions:

1. Were you happy during your stay in an American institution of higher learning?

2. Were the members of the college faculty, administration, and students kindly disposed?

3. Do you think you rendered a real service, and if so of what nature?

4. Have you any general comments you would like to share with us?

Please note that *no names or identifying data* will be used in connection with any excerpts which we may publish, unless you expressly authorize us to do so.

Cordially yours,
STEPHEN DUGGAN, *Chairman*
Emergency Committee in Aid of Displaced Foreign Scholars

The displaced scholars wrote for the most part enthusiastically and usually with keen discernment about their experiences in American colleges and universities. Many stated they had learned as much from their students as they had imparted, and spoke of the "patience" with which their first efforts to lecture in the English language had been received. Their contributions to American curricula were described modestly. Often scientific achievements of a high order received less space than a proud account by a scholar of a college yearbook which had been dedicated to him. Their good will and sense of participation in American academic life were unmistakable. They wrote with tolerance of situations both good and bad which they had encountered, and in general evidenced a breadth of understanding and humanity which gave eloquent promise for their future as citizens of our university world.

The following letter is from a successful displaced scholar now in one of the smaller progressive universities in the eastern part of the country. It is one of the most thoughtful and objective summaries by a displaced scholar of adjustment in American academic life that we have received:

Thank you very much for your letter of November 9. I am very glad to be asked for a summing up of my experiences in

United States university life during the early stages of adjustment in the process of which the Committee played such a helpful role.

You probably are aware of the fact that trouble and success in each case may have been due to the personal approach of the foreign scholar. Thus in my own case the fact that I left Germany on my own free decision relatively late, after trying experiences under the Nazi regime when hope of a breakdown of the regime without foreign interference was gone, certainly had some bearing on my readiness to adjust myself to the new environment. I am very much aware of the fact that it has played a role in making me feel more at ease and happy from the very beginning and in spite of occasional setbacks which might have irritated me otherwise.

Another fact which may have contributed towards individual differences in adjustment is the age of the refugee. On the one side the capacity for adjustment declines almost parallel to the years of age, and on the other hand the outlook on life changes basically with each decade; ambitions and expectations as to the professional career are frequently less prominent in the mind of a mature person. The destruction of European culture has brought about in many of us a state of resignation, in which the continued pursuit of professional activity appeared meaningless. Although such a state of mind may have sometimes handicapped initiative, it may on the other side have enabled some of us more, in accepting with a sense of humor a new situation and strange standards in another country.

My personal experiences in this country have been relatively fortunate. Following the advice and active assistance of the American Friends Service Committee I went to Middlewest seemed to offer a better chance with less competition among refugees and a greater readiness to accept newcomers. It has proven to be true for the school as well as the community. People have been very friendly, helpful, and cooperative, although the townspeople in later years—after the United States entered the war—have partly set us apart with a certain suspicion and prejudice. The group of professional people with whom I was associated have been extremely kind to me and my two boys during the whole time of my stay. They accepted me as a member of their group in every respect and without any reservation; always shall I remember them gratefully. The progress I made in my academic work was mainly due to the attitude of the head of the department. I feel that he really deserves the merit for the successful solution of my academic problem in this country. First, I am sure that without his moral support as well as his actual appointment during my early visit in 1939 I never would have succeeded in getting a start. Later too, he handled the situation with broadmindedness, imagination, and elasticity as I never met again in any college office. On the contrary, later contacts have repeatedly illustrated to me the singularity of his way of dealing with people and developing his teaching staff. It seems to me that the final success for refugees depended to a considerable extent on these unpredictable personal contacts. I consider that I started to work as a stroke of good luck.

The attitude of the college administration on the other hand, was decidedly difficult. Anti-foreign sentiments prevailed from the beginning, they developed strongly during the war and prohibited finally my being accepted as a regular faculty member. I feel that the only reason for accepting me at all for a transitional period was due to the financial advantage on account of the grants given by the Emergency Committee. I also feel that they occasionally took advantage of the situation. The chances of being accepted on an equal basis with American competitors after the period of transition have been improved by the shortage of teachers during the war. Without the many vacancies and the shifting of personnel through the war booms, possibilities of getting settled would have been less favorable. A return to peacetime conditions may reverse the development to some extent, especially in cases where refugees did not yet succeed to get a tenure. A certain hesitancy to accept European scholars without discrimination continues to exist and tends to weigh into their disfavor after the first stage of curiosity has worn out.

The acceptance by the students was very favorable; I have the impression that they all were very anxious to become acquainted with teachers of European background, that they enjoyed the different approach and the wider experience we had to offer. This became particularly apparent after the United States became involved in the war. In contrast to the reaction of the community in general, students were after the war started all the more interested in getting direct information about European problems and especially Germany's conflicts.

The question as to whether I feel I have rendered real service to this country is difficult to answer because it depends on what is considered the ultimate aim of professional work in the field. My recent contributions in terms of research papers or speeches are only a few and almost negligible in their general importance. The more lasting contribution in the scholastic field, it seems to me, lies with the intangible influence European refugees had by offering a different approach and different methods in dealing with problems of the social sciences. Some American scholars are very much aware of over-departmentalization and the lack of integration in this country. To have strengthened the interest in a more comprehensive approach by continuously forcing the issue in discussions seems to me one of our lasting services, the result of which, however, may only become visible in the long run without being traceable to one or the other individual. The immediate response of American colleagues has been clearly divided into two opposites. We have had the most gratifying acknowledgments by those who by themselves had already been interested in developing new approaches in the social science fields. Those, however, who accepted American standards unquestioningly, rather resent any interference and expect refugees who want to have a fair competitive chance to adjust their standards completely to the deeply entrenched traditions in colleges and universities.

Herein lie the roots of any trouble and complications we may expect in the future. Those of us who, as myself, came to this country in an advanced stage of life, will always remain foreign. This is our chance as well as our handicap. I feel clearly that after the war the handicap will weigh more heavily than the chances which during the war have been extraordinary because during the ordeal doubts in the value of established patterns and readiness for changes have been uppermost.

These are, in a summary fashion, my professional experiences in the United States. I hope the survey answers your questions adequately. I shall be glad to elaborate on any point if you wish.

A letter from a displaced scholar who had experience in three universities and was finally called to an important position in one of the departments of the United States government contains this statement:

I was very happy during my stay in American institutions of higher learning. As Research Fellow as well as later Lecturer and Research Associate, I considered it a great honor and a great opportunity to be associated with such institutions.

Each of these institutions had its special attraction. Members of the college faculties, administration, and students were 90 per cent kindly disposed. The vast majority were extremely friendly and helpful. In those instances in which faculty members were reluctant to recommend my courses to students, it was not because they were unkindly disposed to me. It was rather that they hesitated to recommend elective courses which would require additional work in preparation. I learned of many faculty members who recommended my courses to students because of the favorable reports they had received from students who had taken them.

I think that I rendered a real service by offering in lectures as well as in publications a new approach to the subject matters involved. This approach was sometimes comparative, which means my European background of experience permitted comparisons which otherwise would not have been possible. Sometimes the more philosophical approach based on my European training, with its greater emphasis in the humanities, enabled the students to gain a broader aspect on problems discussed. I do not hesitate to say, however, that I received at least as many incentives and suggestions in my teaching experience from those whom I taught. The interruption of lectures by questions was new to me. It made me aware of the more practical and democratic spirit of the American system of education and the American way of life in general. Without this experience in my classes, I probably would not have understood as readily the system of administration in American government, of which I am now a part. I was gratified to see my ideas take root, developed, and copied by my students as well as by readers of my publications. Occasionally, however, it was disturbing to discover that sometimes this went to an extreme—that there was not enough respect before another man's spiritual property.

Generally speaking, I feel the Emergency Committee in Aid of Displaced Foreign Scholars made an outstanding and unusual contribution. I was most impressed by the unselfish active interest of individual members of the Committee as well as by the spirit of the group as a whole. You were not merely interested in seeing that we had the means of a livelihood; you *worked* to see that that livelihood would give us a chance to use our capabilities to our own best interests and that of our adopted country. We were broken and degraded in spirit, having been chased all over the world. Your efforts helped to restore in us not only self-confidence and self-respect, but what to us seemed to be even more vital, faith in humanity. You gave us a dignified place from which we could start a new life. It strengthened our courage to still find a group of men, such as your Committee, who do not complacently take freedom and democracy for granted, but are ever on the alert to guard and maintain a spirit of good will, cooperativeness, justice, and equality among men. Not only have those scholars you have directly helped benefited from your work but also all displaced scholars in this country. Because of what you have done for us, I as well as the others you have helped feel that in gratitude we shall do whatever is possible to serve our country. I only hope that your work and the spirit in which it was done will be a guide for future generations, so that situations such as we have witnessed shall never recur.

This letter is from a distinguished mathematician now in one of the midwestern universities:

Since my arrival in this country [March, 1939] I am associated with the Mathematics Department of the University and I can assert that I am completely satisfied with my stay and my work here. The members of the departmental faculty gave me, from the beginning, the kindest help in adjusting myself to life and educational traditions of this country. I was fortunate enough to establish the best relations, scientifically as well as personally, to them and to find quite a number of real friends.

At any occasion, the members of the University faculty and administration showed an extremely kind disposition towards me. Also with our students I got along very well, during my classes as well as in personal relations. For elementary and in advanced teaching I always found the best cooperation and interest.

Since 1939 I participated in our normal teaching schedule with a full-time load of both undergraduate and graduate courses. Whether I did render so a real service to our University is not up to me to decide. However, you may find an indication of the University's judgment in the fact that I got a five years' appointment as a full professor of Mathematics this fall.

There is only one general comment I should like to share with you. With all the greatest appreciation I have for the work of the Emergency Committee and for the generous help it has given to so many of us refugees, I cannot but regret that with the termination of its work it has left one problem unsolved. I have in mind the situation of the relatively small group of scholars whose age did not let them find a sort of permanent position in this country and who, now or pretty soon, have to live under hard conditions. I wonder whether your broad experience could see a way to help them. Mostly they are lawfully entitled to get "pensions" from Germany which, of course, are not paid and probably cannot be paid directly now. However, inasmuch as the amount needed is not large at all, compared with other claims against Germany, could it not be made possible to use a small part of the German assets in this country for an emergency action for those men?

I am glad to have an opportunity to express my personal thanks for the great work you and your Committee have done.

The following letter is from a Nobel Prize Winner in Physics now teaching in one of our great universities in the Middle West:

I feel, and always have felt, very happy to be a professor at an American university.

I have always had the best of relations with members of the college faculty and the students, and only once did I find an administrative officer with whom I could not get along.

I hope that I am of some service in teaching and research. During the period of the war, I was engaged in war work.

I like especially the fact that the different fields (at least in the larger universities with which I have been associated) are not represented by only one full-time professor but rather by a group of coordinated men, an arrangement that permits healthy competition and cross-fertilization of ideas. The great power put in the hands of university presidents was somewhat astonishing to me. Actually universities in Germany before the Nazis came to power were in that respect more democratic. More frequent exchange of personnel between different universities would, according to my personal impression, be an advantage for the general progress in scientific and educational fields.

The following letter is from a displaced scholar in one of the great universities of the Pacific coast:

I am glad to have the opportunity in reply to your letter to express once more my gratitude for the help given to me by the Emergency Committee.

I shall be glad to answer your four questions:

I was very happy indeed during my stay in every one of the universities and seminaries with which I have been affiliated through the years since 1937—far happier, I should say, than ever in the country of my birth. I felt that I fitted better into the cosmopolitan and broad-minded spirit of American institutions, which all gave me splendid opportunities to work in my field and according to my special research interests.

I have found a far heartier welcome everywhere than a foreigner could possibly expect. Even during the war, while still, technically speaking, an "enemy alien," I have never felt anything but unprejudiced cooperation and personal friendliness on the part of the student body and, with one single inconsequential exception, also among the entire faculty.

The high amount of praise which my work and my teaching has met everywhere is, I think, not only due to the agreeable American politeness but has been rather genuine in most cases. I also believe that my approach, particularly in my field of study, has been a real contribution for which there was need on the part of the students who have come in large numbers (last time more than 100) to this unrequired course.

I think, however, this request would not be quite complete if I would not add, confidentially, my opinion that in spite of obvious successes it seems to be extremely hard for a foreigner ever to get on equal footing with an American as far as position and salary is concerned, if there is not a personal influential connection available. After eight years of work I find myself today harder struggling in financial respect than ever before.

A distinguished scientist in one of the leading universities of the eastern coast writes as follows:

Was I happy during my stay?—Very, very much, from the first day to the present day. Everybody was (or, at least, seemed to be) kindly disposed towards me, helped me in every way, and several real friendships developed with my colleagues at the museum where I work. I came here after waiting for my visa in London for a year; I had been allowed to work in the museum in London, even after it was closed when war broke out; my British colleagues were kind, but the difference in personal approach was overwhelming when I came here; in London I had to earn my living outside my profession—here, I got a salary from the Emergency Committee at once. Even now it strikes me as wonderful that a questionnaire asks me whether I am *happy;* I don't believe that could happen anywhere in the world except in this country.

Did I render a real service? . . . How can I answer this question myself? I published papers written in the museum. I am collaborating on a big bibliographical enterprise of my department, and perhaps that is a real service that I am doing the Italian part, since nobody else is familiar with that language. I suppose I have rendered a real service to the College, helping out, with rather sudden appointments in emergencies arising there (more students than expected, somebody going on leave), as an instructor in zoology.

General comments? If the Emergency Committee had not helped me, I could not have taken up again the research work I had done in Germany but would have had to earn my living some other way, and probably forever, because I got started here as a palaeontologist only through being in the museum.

The following letter is from an eminent scholar in one of the great universities of the eastern coast:

I am indeed very glad to answer your questions about my reaction to the situation which I met while a member of the staff of an American institution of higher learning.

I have been happy during the more than eleven years of my stay.

The members of the graduate school as well as of the undergraduate faculty, administration, and students, have always been kindly disposed. I have won many friends among the faculty and there is not one member of the Fine Arts faculty with whom I have other than cordial relations. With the students I have very enjoyable relations. Some of them have come back to my courses for several years, a number have worked or are working on their master thesis and a few on their Ph.D. thesis with me.

I hope that I have rendered some service to the University. I have tried to learn from my American colleagues,—among which there are some of the highest scholarship,—their method of teaching, and I have tried to combine with the American methods whatever I have learned during my European training and teaching. I have added some courses which were not given before.

I believe that other displaced foreign scholars will feel as I do: The help of the Emergency Committee and the American colleagues have made me feel the obligation to work as hard as I can for my new country and to bring out the best possible results in my own work and in the work of the young American students who are to carry on the torch which has been spent in Europe.

A displaced scholar in one of our midwestern universities makes this statement:

It is with pleasure that I am answering your kind letter of November 9th. On the termination of the Emergency Committee in Aid of Displaced Foreign Scholars, I wish to express my appreciation of its excellent work.

I have been connected with several American institutions of higher learning in the past twelve years and met everywhere with the utmost courtesy and understanding.

The members of college faculties, the administration and the students were kind, and eager to cooperate.

I have had many students who entered a successful scientific career. I published about forty articles and a book and feel that my work was useful and a real contribution.

I am sure the history of the Emergency Committee will be a cultural document, and I am deeply interested in the forthcoming book.

The following letter is from a leading scholar in one of the great universities of the eastern coast:

I was—and am—happy to be affiliated with various American institutions of higher learning.

The members of the various faculties and the administrations in question were kindly disposed. The students I have taught were most generous in expressing their appreciation of my work, and many have remained in close personal contact with me.

I believe I have been able to make some contribution to the development of health service in this country, to judge from the many letters and personal comments I have received from the leaders in the field.

I have developed a research and teaching program in the social and economic aspects of medicine and organization and administration of medical care, a field hitherto little touched in this country. At present I am in charge of a series of lectures for undergraduate medical students, a course on Medical Care in Modern Society for graduate students of public health, and two courses on Community Health Organization for social workers.

Since 1939 I have done much research on organization of health services, and many of my findings were published. The list of my publications in this country up to now contains twelve titles, one of which was prepared for the Office of Strategic Services with which I served about half a year; and a book recently published by the University Press. I should like to mention that many public and voluntary agencies request my service as consultant.

A displaced scholar in a university of the middle Atlantic area writes:

The years during which I have been a member of the staff of the University have been very happy ones. Administrative officers and faculty members have been at all times helpful, friendly, and kindly disposed, and my relations with the students have been cordial and enjoyable.

I think I have rendered a small service by introducing Archives Administration as a field of graduate study and by organizing in our Department of Public Administration an integrated undergraduate program of courses in Record Administration which will help to raise the standards of record administration here at least.

I think I can consider it a testimony of confidence on the part of the administration and of my full-time colleagues that, for the period from September 1, 1945, to August 31, 1946, I have been appointed Dean of the Graduate Division of the School of Social Sciences and Public Affairs of this University.

The following letter is from a displaced scholar in one of the trans-Mississippi universities:

I have very much enjoyed my stay in American colleges and universities and have had great pleasure in my teaching work.

I always experienced much kindness from the members of the college faculty and administration as well as from the students, and with a number of them I have also afterwards remained in friendly contact.

The service which I may have been able to render consists, I should think, besides the general teaching success, in the cultural experiences from abroad which I could bring to the attention and interest of the students. I felt so especially in the teaching in the A.S.T.P. Program, and also in college.

A letter from a displaced scholar in one of the smaller universities of the eastern coast declares:

I have been, and still am, happy as a member of the staff of an American college.

I have met with the kindest consideration from members of the faculty and the administration. My contact with the student body has resulted as most pleasant and satisfactory.

Besides my regular activities as a teacher, I have had the

privilege to offer my modest contribution to the rapprochement and better understanding of Latin America through many lectures to different clubs and other American associations.

I am glad of this opportunity to express once more my gratitude to your Committee. Your assistance on my arrival in the United States has meant a great deal to me, as it helped to adjust myself to this country, enabling me thereby to add my grain of sand to those objectives at which your Committee was aiming.

This letter is from one of the most distinguished scholars in his field teaching in an institution on the eastern coast:

I am happy to learn that you are engaged in writing the history of the Emergency Committee, to which I owe lasting gratitude.

From the day of my landing here back in 1934 till this very day, my connection with   was the source of happiness and inspiration to me. The late President and his successor, the members of its faculties and the student body were always most kindly disposed toward me. In fact, I never felt being an "exile," but was treated first as a welcome guest, and soon afterwards as a regular member of the faculty.

I do hope that American scholarship in general and our institution in particular do not regret having invited me to join their ranks. I am sure you don't wish to embarrass me with question no. 3. My specialty is research. In the course of the last seven years I published a series of seven monographs, four in the Annual, and three in the Journal.

And finally may I assure you that no matter what I shall accomplish in the field of scholarship and pure research, I shall never be able to even partially repay the debt I owe to America with its atmosphere of freedom, and to your Committee, which for the first four crucial years undertook the financial responsibility for my position here.

The following letter is from a displaced scholar in one of the great state universities of the Middle West:

I was and am happy at my place of work, the University. I was treated with extraordinary courtesy and consideration by my colleagues as well as by the administration and the student body.

The third question is, I believe, not for me to answer. I attach a letter of the Chairman of the Department.

I should like to avail myself of this opportunity and say what admirable work the Emergency Committee has done which will not be forgotten in the cultural history of this country.

The letter this scholar enclosed, from his department chairman, is as follows:

On behalf of the University I am happy to state that Dr. has rendered a significant service in his capacity of Professor of Economics. This service has consisted of teaching both graduates and undergraduates, of research and writing, and of various types of public service.

Aside from these contributions, Dr. has brought to the University faculty and student body a goodly measure of Old World culture and learning, which can be supplied only by one with his deep and sympathetic understanding and breadth of scholarship. Dr. has been a good citizen and an honored member of the University community.

From a fine college of the Middle West one of the most successful displaced scholars sends the following letter:

Now I shall take up your questions as they are arranged in your letter:

1) Yes, and more so in the Middle West than in the East, there we were quite a number of Germans. We carefully avoided forming a clique, yet could not help giving the appearance of a kind of special unofficial group within the faculty. I do not know whether our American colleagues considered us as such, I do not even believe that they did; but the mere possibility of their doing so created a slight feeling of uneasiness. Here, where I was the only foreigner, I never felt the same way. I became just a member of the faculty as everybody else and enjoyed teaching and learning unconditionally.

2) Faculty: Yes, and to an extent which was a great surprise for a newcomer from Germany. So much helpfulness as I found

here could never have been expected from a German faculty, if things had been the other way around. Now, after eight years in this country, and being on terms of intimate friendship with American colleagues with whom I was privileged to work in these years, I see that the faculties were more generous than we ever realized in suppressing initial feelings of uneasiness about the mass-intrusion. I know by now that such feelings existed, but they were shown only in the most exceptional cases. No word of praise is high enough for the attitude of the faculties in general: to give the "intruder" a chance and judge him, after a time, on the merits of his work.

Administration: I experienced the kindest understanding for my special problems from all officers of administration, without any exception. It is only now that I realize, in the light of observations made in the preceding paragraph, how much the administrations did, without our knowing it, in order to make our work possible, and successful.

Students: Their attitude was, perhaps, the greatest surprise. I approached my first class with great apprehensions; being a newcomer with a very poor command of language, perfectly unacquainted with the teaching methods of the country, I expected either the ironic smile which I had seen so often in German audiences when a foreign speaker made a mistake in expression, or the cold condescending tolerance with which I had become acquainted in another country. Instead I found the students invariably polite, friendly, attentive, and lenient towards the weakness of a foreigner. I am sure that I seasoned my first lectures with incredible blunders, but I never saw as much as a smile in the audience. From the very beginning I saw that they accepted unusual ways of teaching with serious interest. If I have succeeded in my work here, I have to thank my students no less than my colleagues.

Coming from a large German university I did not think in the beginning that I could be put to good use anywhere but in one of the great American universities. I do not believe so any longer. On the contrary, I feel that people of our type are more useful when distributed among the smaller colleges all over the country.

If the educational system of the country expects an enrichment from the cooperation of immigrants, I believe that it makes better sense to let this new element work through a multiplicity of small channels rather than in large clusters.

An eminent scholar in a great engineering school on the eastern coast offers this comment:

I will be glad to answer the questions of your Emergency Committee which has earned the gratitude of all of us.

1. I was and am happy here.
2. Administration, colleagues and students have made me always feel at home.
3. I have been in war research and development work since 1941, especially in connection with radar, and hope to have done as well as my new country could expect of me.

A German professor is inclined to feel himself more important than he is, to be critical against surroundings not yet fully comprehended and to bank on previous accomplishments which do not count here. If he overcomes this attitude, adaptation has proved easy in all cases I could observe.

This letter is from a scholar in one of the large universities of the eastern coast:

As you may remember, I spent the first three years in this country at   College, and came to   University in 1940. The eight years which I have so far spent in this country have been very happy ones, full of interesting and stimulating experiences. At   College the atmosphere was extraordinarily friendly: everybody in the administration, on the faculty, and in the student body was most kind and helpful, and there was a fine spirit of cooperation which helped me greatly in becoming adjusted to academic habits and traditions in this country. I have also nothing but praise and gratitude for the way in which I have been treated by my colleagues in my own Department here at the University, and while I should probably go too far if I described the feeling toward me in the faculty at large as "friendly" I am anxious to state that I have never met with hostility.

I do hope that I have rendered a real service but feel that it is for other people to pass a judgment on this question. If they are inclined to answer the question in the affirmative I should suggest that the reason might be that I combine a variety of interests and approaches in a way which does not seem to be very common now. However, this is in all probability just an accident, and there is no reason why a native and American-trained classicist should not either now or later represent the same combination of interests.

There is no doubt in my mind that the work of your Committee has been highly beneficial, and I can see the stimulating effect which the absorption of foreign scholars has had wherever I look, yet most particularly in the learned periodicals. Actually, I am at times inclined to regret that it has not been possible to find places for a few more who would have made valuable contributions, and I cannot always approve of the arguments which have been used in rejecting some such candidates. For instance, while I of course fully recognize the right of any given institution to consider a man's capacity of adjusting himself to a new academic environment, I yet believe that at times too much has been made of this question and I think there is evidence that very valuable service has been rendered by persons whom one could hardly regard as "completely adjusted."

The distinguished scholar who writes the following has had experience with two great universities and is now established in one of the universities on the west coast:

Yes. I was very happy during the stay at   University which was made possible in part to me by the Committee's support.

I found the fullest support from the members of the college faculty and the administration, and I had a very good relationship with my students.

My work at the University consisted of various activities. I was a member of the School of International Relations. I did research work which resulted in the publication of a book. This book has been mentioned frequently and quoted by other scholars and has been listed in the last number of the *Far Eastern Quarterly* in an article "Outstanding Recent Books on the Far East" by Meredith Cameron as one of the valuable books in the Far

Eastern field of books. In addition to this research work, I taught in the political science and history departments courses on international relations, international law, and especially Far Eastern subjects. From the comments of my colleagues and the president of the University, I believe that my work was of real value to the University.

I would like to use this occasion to express the feeling of gratitude which I hold for the Committee's assistance in giving me a start in American academic work. At my third year at the University I was taken over by the University, which paid my salary from its funds, and I have since accepted a position with a University where at present I am Associate Professor and Acting Chairman of the Far Eastern Department. I have been able to continue my regular academic career, contributing my part to the development of Far Eastern studies in this country. During the war I worked and directed an Army Specialized Training Program at this University on several Far Eastern countries. The University has had the satisfaction to see that several of the students of this program have done extremely valuable intelligence work in breaking the Japanese code and supplying information to American air and ground forces, which among other things, was solely responsible for the attack on and destruction of two whole Japanese convoys.

In the meantime I have become an American citizen and hope to be able to give all my efforts to contributing to the development of work in my field in this country where I have found a new home and where such contribution has been welcome.

The able scholar who writes the following was absorbed into our government service at the close of the war:

I was very happy during my stay in American institutions of higher learning. The college faculty and my students were very kindly disposed towards me. In fact my teaching was regarded as an unusual success. However, I know from the administration that there is no way to overcome vested interests, especially in conservative schools.

The services were regarded as of unusual nature, especially during wartime, since I had to teach subjects connected with the war effort. I met hundreds of my former students in Europe, some as occupational administrators, intelligence officers, etc.

The number of European scholars who will get a permanent job in American universities will be very low. Primarily jobs financed by outside sources will be available. Maybe then my grandchildren will belong to a group which will fight for their vested interests against the newcomers of the 21st century.

You might be interested to know that I am the only European scholar connected with the Prosecution of the Major Axis War Criminals as a member of the American staff of prosecution. I have been in Nürnberg for quite a while and enjoy my present activities.

From a scholar in the field of law comes this comment:

Teaching in the United States seemed to me more difficult and challenging a proposition than it was in Europe. Whether or not the students ask questions expressly, one always has the feeling that they are asking the teacher, or at least themselves, What good is their learning to them? I also have the feeling that they rely on the authority of the teacher much less than this was the case in educational institutions elsewhere. The reason of authority is, for them, much less than the authority of a good reason. I repeat, I am not sure that this is a typical experience. But it is one of the main reasons that enable me to answer your first question so emphatically in the affirmative.

A scholar now teaching in a great university on the west coast writes:

I was (and still am) very happy as a member of the faculty of an American university. My colleagues were in the great majority kindly disposed, likewise the administration, and particularly so the student body.

I think that I rendered a service in opening the Universities of   and   to musicology. I see in the fact that   University has engaged after my leaving there another musicologist an indirect admission that the field of musicology has been recognized. Also here, our department has been granted the right to bestow the Ph.D. in Musicology a year after my arrival.

I should like to stress again the hospitality and cordiality with which I have been received. The administration was grateful for the opportunity, afforded by the Emergency Committee, to make use of my services. Only very rarely have I heard criticism to the effect that foreign scholars were an unfair competition to American scholars. These people did not realize that, if the Emergency Committee had not supplied funds, nobody would have held the positions.

The writer of the following interesting suggestion has become one of the most successful teachers in his field:

As for the fourth question: If I may avail myself of a legal term, I would say that the statute of limitations must be applied to the status of an immigrant labeled "refugee." When I arrived in New York on August 18, 1938, my first act was to ask for the address of the Federal District Court in order to file my first papers immediately. Thus, I filed them within twenty-four hours after my arrival. I was granted the privilege of being an American citizen on February 3, 1944. When the "I Am an American Day" followed the latter day on the third Sunday of May, 1944, I was honored by being selected to deliver the address on behalf of the new citizens. Thus, I think the time has come to drop the designation "refugee" with respect to people of my class. Such a label might be all right for European politicians who came here only for the purpose of awaiting the downfall of Hitlerism and Mussolinism and then to return to their former profession.

People like me, who have become American lawyers and have completely severed the ties with their former countries, want to be recognized, not only in law but also in fact, as Americans. Carl Schurz was a refugee only in the first few years of his presence in this country. Would someone have dared to call the later Secretary of the Interior and the United States Senator a refugee? If one can become an American citizen after five years, this means that having become a citizen one has ceased to be a "refugee." One concept is not compatible with the other concept. In view of this, I would suggest to drop the words "refugee professors" and to replace it by the words "professors and teachers who immigrated into this country," or if there were professors who did not intend to become Americans, to separate my class from the latter one in the terminology.

A writer and research worker offers this comment:

I am glad to say that I was happy during my stay in the American institution where I did teaching or research work. I liked especially the attitude of the students who were so willing to learn and take every advice from me and who were so patient with my imperfect pronunciation of the English language during the first years.

However, I cannot deny that the attitude of some American scholars of my own generation was not always as friendly as I had expected. I am not able to decide whether the reason lies in the possible difference between American and European mentality or in an uneasy feeling about the invasion of so many Europeans, or in both of these instances. However, the majority of the American scholars were very friendly and were of great assistance to me.

One scholar has a special word to offer about students:

As to students, I can only say that their reaction has been 100 per cent positive from the beginning. Their readiness to listen to lectures certainly during the first years, which must have been a torture to them from the point of view of linguistic performance, has been extraordinary. They have invariably shown enthusiasm and eagerness to learn and absorb new ideas, and mostly they did so in full understanding that the ideas were, naturally, connected with some foreign stamp and alien background. There is hardly a single case I can remember when during these ten years a student has given evidence that he or she resented the teaching of a foreign-born professor. On the other hand, a number of most pleasant and gratifying personal friendships have developed in my case from my contacts with students.

From a midwestern institution comes the following statement:

I feel that in my case the support I have received from you was decisive; it may very well have made the difference between success and failure. I have by now achieved a permanent position on this campus to which you first sent me and should like to think that I have also succeeded in establishing a certain reputation through my contributions to a field (philosophy) to which I have long tended, but which I did not formally enter before I came to this country. My bibliography since 1939, when I received your aid, has well over twenty items.

Perhaps I should also mention that I have in the meantime become a citizen, and that I am married to a native American. As a wartime contribution I worked, virtually in addition to my regular load, in the A.S.T.P. (Foreign Area Studies Program).

The reception with which I met here on the part of faculty and students was generally very friendly, in many cases exceedingly cordial and hospitable.

A distinguished scientist who has divided his time between the East and the Middle West, states:

I certainly was and am happy in my relations with University and the University of   . In the beginning it was naturally somewhat hard for me to get adjusted to the different set-up of American institutions of higher learning as compared with European experiences with respect to the more practical and businesslike nature of college administrations, the much stricter treatment of students (very frequent elementary examinations, roll calls, etc.).

The members of the faculty, administration and student body were extremely kindly disposed. Perhaps this is partly due to the fact that I tried hard to mentally become just a normal member of the staff as soon as possible and to avoid to be an exceptional case in any respect. I have known other cases where the adjustment was much harder and the response of the faculty and students much less favorable, due to the newcomers' efforts to secure higher salaries before the administration could know what the merits of the individuals concerned would be with respect to the aims of the particular college, or due to open arrogance of some newcomers as to their cultural background. Another possible factor in my favor here was my sincere Catholic faith.

I would like to state that in my opinion one of the most important tasks for a man of academic background who comes to

this country in relatively mature years and is in the beginning
bewildered by the difference in American and European outlook on life, set of values, etc., is to try to understand the historical reasons for these differences. In other words he has to
learn systematically by reading, observation, and thinking. If he
does not, he will become thoroughly unhappy and, what is worse,
a nuisance. This does by no means mean that he should pretend
to believe that everything is better here than in Europe. However,
with sincerity and good will towards American institutions he
will gain the respect of his colleagues and he will be much more
able to afford frankness without hurting anybody's feelings.

This letter is from a displaced scholar who has had experience in a great eastern and an equally great midwestern university:

I consider myself extremely fortunate in that the University of
            invited me, as early as 1933, to come to this country
and to lecture on psychology. After a relatively short period of
adjustment I have been very happy in all institutions with which
I was affiliated. Most of the members of the faculty of each of
these colleges accepted me with kindness and generosity. I was
given generously freedom of work and of teaching; colleagues
and students alike very patiently tried to understand the sometimes strange and awkward ways of the German professor. It
was my good fortune to find friends wherever I went; some of
them proved to be more faithful than I ever have known, even
those I left behind me in Europe.

I would say that the intellectual relationship between myself
and the people I came in contact with was of the nature of "give-
and-take." When I came to this country I was quite unaware of
many basic problems of my own science, problems that are deeply
rooted in the American way of life. At that time I did not realize
the full scope of the often-stated difference in the attitudes of
American and Continental psychology toward the relation between theory and facts. German psychology appears to be biased
toward (speculative) theory, American psychology toward technology and critical accumulation of facts. Through this understanding, I believe, I have attained a more healthy, more bal-
anced attitude in my work and my teaching. My service, if any,

I see in my passing on this new insight; I endeavor to teach American students that facts without theory are blind, and theories without facts, empty. A number of European scholars in this country seem to have gone the same way as I did and met with similar experiences. It is probably partly due to this influence that the conviction among the American students seems to grow that scientific endeavor has small virtue without the consistent, living intent toward integration.

This letter is from a displaced scholar who is successfully teaching in a municipal institution:

About your first question, whether I was happy during my stay in an American institution of higher learning, I may say that I never looked at any of the places I filled as just a stay. Since I finally acquired citizenship about a year ago, I know now for certain that my outlook was the right one: I felt at home and was eager to show it. My answer therefore would definitely be: Yes. Of course, a number of circumstances like the small-town atmosphere of my first position, the friendly Y.M.C.A. spirit in the second, the attractive living conditions of my present whereabouts have contributed very substantially. And yet all this would not have been enough if I had not liked to teach at college. I am also aware that I did not bring along all the ballast of a person who looks back and never unpacks his coffers. Naturally I have definite opinions on my European experience, both German and English; but they mean only one thing to me in retrospect: I am sure that I did right to try to come over. I got what I wanted when I needed it most.

As to the second question, how faculty, administration, and students acted towards me, I am particularly impressed by the reception that the respective faculties, chairmen and colleagues alike, gave me, and certainly the attitude of the student body has always been most gratifying. As to the chairmen of the departments in which I worked, it will give you some idea of my close personal ties, when I say that I made it a point to name them all as my personal sponsors when time came for my naturalization. The first one of them is actually and literally responsible for my coming to this country, and with the second one there remain the finest friendship ties my wife and I have ever known. That incidentally goes for a number of other colleagues in the Middle West as well as here in New York. As to the student body, I want to say what a lift it has always given to me to find interest and eagerness beyond the classroom. The ease of American college contacts compares very favorably with other memories of mine.

The third question, whether I rendered real service, has been cautiously framed by you as "whether I think so" or not. In my own mind I am quite sure that I did, witness the student response and the relations with the colleagues. The nature of that service I would simply call conscientious performance in class. In no way do I think that differed from what others contribute every day. To meet that standard continually has been the source of my greatest inner satisfaction, be that in the routine of required freshman courses, or be it in the electives which I had the good fortune to teach. Since you are more keenly aware of the troubles that many a newcomer to America may have faced when teaching survey courses, it will interest you to hear my considered opinion that I am more and more convinced of them the longer I teach them. True that in some cases it may have been my good luck to draw on life memories or knowledge of geography that enabled me to enliven an otherwise too condensed presentation of subjects that to the student seemed remote or bookish. But to turn specialist knowledge to good use has revealed to me the nature of college education: it bridges the gulf between the general public and the ivory tower specialist.

Under your fourth question—namely, possible further comment on related matters—I would like to point out that with all the strenuous work that college teaching implies (and I have not yet met a single European who realized that fact before he set foot on American soil) it has always been possible for me to keep up some research. Besides, as college usually functions within some community set-up, I have been called upon to lecture and broadcast for the institution at which I was, and that has certainly reassured me on the same subject that I hinted at in the foregoing paragraph: the American college is the answer to the danger in modern civilization that overspecialization atomizes society.

I hope that these remarks tell you that one man appreciates his "Vita Nuova."

A natural scientist states:

It is a great pleasure for me to answer the questions about my reaction in my new position at our Museum, for these reactions belong to the most wonderful I ever had in life.

I felt and still am feeling completely happy in my position here, both on account of the kind of work I am doing and the mental attitude my superiors are showing toward my work, and on account of the "group spirit" among our staff which included me very shortly after my arrival here.

Everybody here, ranging from the President of our Museum and the director, the chief curator and my fellow curators down to the technical and clerical employees, was perfectly friendly and understanding, and this nice atmosphere has never been troubled. In the course of time, an intimate friendship between some of my fellow curators and the chief curator on one side and me on the other has arisen, a friendship which is extending even to our families.

From what my superior and friend, the chief curator, told me only a few weeks ago, I have to assume that part of my work here is considered to be a real service to our institution; maybe my European background with the linguistic knowledge and experience which is needed over there, furnished me with some abilities which are higher appreciated here than they would be in Europe.

The only comment I have to offer, is, that I am happy to have become a citizen of a country which has produced such an institution, both humane and scientific at the same time, as was the Emergency Committee in Aid of Displaced Foreign Scholars.

From the Middle West comes a reassuring statement:

As to your questions, let me answer them one by one: I was and still am very happy as a teacher of musicology at an American university. Whatever dimmed, for a short or long period of time, this happiness of teaching I shared with my American-born colleagues.

Of the three groups you list, the most rewarding was the students. Not once did I feel or sense any anti-Semitism or any other form of prejudice among the students whom I taught for eight years. I also found my colleagues generally most friendly and understanding. Those in the fields of Music, Literature, Fine Arts, and Modern Language frequently became my closest friends.

It is because of the response of the students and the understanding of those colleagues who as friends and scholars really matter that teaching remains a pleasure and gratifying responsibility. I do not believe that seen as a whole the "plight" of the émigré teacher is greater than that of the average American teacher. The problems of our profession, originating usually with the administration, have been well summed up in Mr. Barzun's book *Teacher in America*.

A distinguished European scholar declares:

It would be inadequate to state that the task of becoming a regular member of the teaching staff of an American institution of higher learning is an easy one for a foreign-born scientist. Of course, the end result is gratifying only in the case of some degree of success, and it may be expected to be somehow proportional to the efforts required by the task. The greatest obstacle to be overcome is the language difficulty.

From Washington comes this statement:

It seems beyond doubt that both the European and the American students have had some profit from their intellectual get-together. The atmosphere has mostly been friendly; judging from an almost three years' collaboration with American-born intellectuals in a government office it seems to me that our services are appreciated and the American government and people have derived some profit from the process of intellectual cross-fertilization.

This comment comes from a foreign scholar in the metropolitan area:

What has bothered me and, I think, other European scholars as well has been the relatively low level of undergraduate work and in some cases even graduate work. On the other hand, I have found American students very intelligent and well able to develop quickly. That is, the starting point is lower but the pick-up is quicker here than in Europe, as far as generalization is possible.

The members of college faculties, administration, and students have, on the whole, all been kindly disposed. In the areas outside the New York concentration, their attitude has been a mixture of sympathy and pride (to have scholars from distant parts of the world on their faculty). In some cases, indeed, outward friendliness has fooled Europeans, who tend to confuse good manners with genuine sympathy and who expect hostility to be open. Personally, I have found it far easier to establish satisfactory professional relations than to establish social contacts. I believe, however, that such difficulties have far more to do with anti-Semitism than with alien-phobia. I should like to stress again that my experiences, despite the qualifications mentioned, have on the whole been very favorable indeed.

While the integration of European scholars into American higher education has been rather successful in general, as far as I can see, there have undoubtedly been serious adjustment difficulties for some of these scholars. The language barrier was, relatively, a minor source of trouble. An arrogant or tactless attitude has in some cases been the almost inevitable overcompensation of complexes acquired through humiliation abroad. On the other hand, I have found that even Americans with liberal ideas and international background are extremely sensitive toward any criticism of American institutions or habits (from the Constitution to boogie-woogie) by foreign-born persons, even if the latter are American citizens. In short, senility on the one side has often had a head-on clash with immaturity on the other. To avoid such pitfalls a continuing process of adjustment and education is indispensable.

From New England comes this comment:

I should like to compare my experiences at a big university and a middle-sized college. The research facilities of the university, of course, are insuperable, but the life in a country college is more stimulating through the much closer personal contact with students and faculty. I have attended more lectures, concerts, and discussions at   College than at

University. In a big place one is more of a number, in a smaller place more of an individuality.

A well known displaced mathematician observes:

I believe that in my field the influx of European scholars had a deep and remaining effect on American institutions. Not only did it improve and intensify the graduate work in Mathematics in many institutions but also it influenced the general attitude of mathematicians concerning theoretical and applied knowledge. Mathematics in the United States before 1930 was rather theoretical without much interest for applications. In the last ten years, especially during the war, this has changed.

In spite of close collaboration of American scholars of American and European background, there is still considerable confusion about the aims, common features, and diversities of American and European universities and secondary schools. I notice this again in France. In many instances I see here the ignorance of my fellow teachers from the United States about European institutions and vice versa.

Exchange of young university teachers (perhaps also secondary school teachers) between the United States and various European schools should be resumed and if possible intensified as soon as normal traveling and living conditions return. This is a vital affair for international understanding and for the improvement of our teaching standards.

From a woman's college in the Middle West comes this statement of a displaced scholar:

While I wish to express my wholehearted appreciation of the great humanitarian work done by so many individuals in this country as well as by such organizations as the Emergency Committee, the New School, and others, and while I wish to stress the friendly attitude shown myself and, as far as I was able to observe, others, once we had been admitted to faculties, I frankly find it hard to conceal my deep disappointment with the general attitude shown the immigrant scholar by many. It manifests itself not only in the frequent open hostility, which often goes far beyond the justifiable concern for native interests and the understandable preference for the American-born candidate. What is far more depressing is the frequent lack of understanding—even with the most well-meaning friends—for our desire, not simply to make a living, but to be in a position to continue our scholarly research for its own sake. For that we are scolded for harboring "European prejudices" or not showing sufficient adaptation to the American democratic principles! This attitude, even more than plain antagonism, is—though often unintentionally—discouraging and humiliating and is what sometimes makes it indeed hard for a scholar to convince himself that he chose wisely in selecting America for his new home—in spite of all that can certainly be said in favor of this choice.

I trust that you will not find me ungrateful when I frankly express these feelings. In making only this comment, I do not mean to disregard the brighter side. But I felt that it might be useful to state, even somewhat bluntly, what seems to be the reason why no class of immigrants seems to have more difficulties in adjusting itself than the European scholar. I do not think that I am telling you anything you have not long been familiar with. But there are still many, and among them very friendly disposed Americans, who apparently do not fully realize this situation, and therefore it seems to me that it cannot be stated often enough.

A letter from the South contains these statements:

"Were you happy during your stay in an American institution of higher learning?" Without reservation, I can answer this question with "Yes." May I add that this happiness extends into the present time and, very likely, will stay with me into the future, since I am now a "permanent member" of the faculty.

"Were the members of the college faculty, administration, and students kindly disposed?" Most assuredly so. My relations with the rest of the faculty, the administration, and last not least, the students have been most friendly and undisturbed. As an illustration of my relations with the student body, I may mention that the students themselves have given recognition to our friendly relations by dedicating last year, their yearbook to me. That is, in itself, a great honor.

"Do you think you rendered a real service, and if so of what nature?" Of course, I realize that this question should be answered rather by the administration than by myself. In fact, President   believes that broad background and thorough training in the various branches of economics is valuable for the kind of job to be done in a liberal arts college with economics as one major field of study. It enables me to teach all courses offered in the department, ranging from courses in general economics to special courses such as labor problems, money and banking, public finance, business management, accounting, etc., etc., a total of around fifteen courses, offered on an alternating schedule device.

The President feels that my general cultural background and my knowledge of various cultures and countries is a specific asset to a liberal arts college. My rooting in the German culture, he feels, is enriching and valuable in that it broadens the outlook of others.

My special training and experience is in music which has, throughout my whole life, been my avocation. As an experienced cellist and ensemble player, I have established for myself a reputation in the state and have guided students' activities in the field: by forming ensemble groups (instrumental and vocal) on the campus, to whom I introduced the priceless treasures of European secular and sacred music especially adapted for smaller ensembles (Collegium Musicum).

This letter is from a displaced scholar in a midwestern university:

I have been at   University for more than seven years now as a Lecturer in the Department of Philosophy and have greatly enjoyed my cooperation with both graduate and undergraduate students. These have been blissful years to me as far as my academic teaching and scholarly work are concerned.

I cannot praise highly enough the friendship of my colleagues and the good spirit of almost all my students. It is almost unavoidable that the difference in the background between the American scholar and the European one limits somewhat the naïve intimacy of their social intercourse. These limits, however, became almost unnoticeable in my case; there has never been any disturbance in the excellent relations and the close cooperation between the other members of my Department and myself; with most of them I am on terms of real friendship. The Chairman of the Department feels and acts like my own father. I was fortunate to establish similar relations with people in other Departments, too. My students love and respect me; and I have been in correspondence with many of them for years.

It is different as regards the Administration. When I joined the Department in 1938, there was no vacancy, and no regular position could be given to me. In the following years, at first, the financial position of the University and, later on, the war which could not but deplete our Department (though not quite as much as many other Philosophical Departments) did not allow a change in the character of my appointment. It was understood, however, and unofficially promised that, at least, I would be made a regular member of the staff and practically the successor to Professor   at the time of his retirement next year. The proposal for the increase of my salary ($3,000) and my promotion—proposals made both by the Department and the Faculty—meet, however, with the obstinate resistance of the President of the University.

I hope that I rendered some service to my students (a) through my being rooted in an intellectual tradition with which most of them were not so well acquainted, partly because they were not familiar with the ancient and modern languages in which it is expressed; (b) as a representative of the   movement which gains more and more ground in France and other countries while it is not yet so well known in the United States; (c) by trying to set an example of a philosophical life, undaunted in spite of persecution and difficulties of all kinds, and never a mere victim of outer events and inner passions.

This letter comes from a displaced scholar in a southern college:

It is very difficult to answer your first question, as my answer depends to an overwhelming extent upon myself, and not so much upon the institutions of higher learning. To summarize my own experience, however, I have been very happy to teach and work in an American institution of higher learning. The differences proved to be a challenge to me, as I have already taught for about twenty years in a different European system.

I am sure that the administration (president and dean), also all the members of the faculty with whom I came in touch and all my students, were very kindly disposed toward me. In all the six years there never have been any serious misunderstandings or difficulties between the college community and me. On the contrary, especially during the war years and before I got my citizenship papers, I felt protected by the college.

I think I have rendered a real service here, but I hope you will check this with the President of the institution. This College had the opportunity to acquire my services as a language teacher who teaches his own language. Then, in a cautious way, I have tried to improve the teaching procedure. The basis of the improvement was my knowledge of the matter, plus a study of the techniques in my field developed by American teachers in other American places of higher learning. I studied them in scholarly magazines, books, etc.—a thrilling experience. Such a progress, however, could be achieved by every new teacher interested in his field, not only by a foreigner. Where I was even more successful, I succeeded in breaking down the barriers between the different departments of my division. This year, when the chairman of my division went on leave, I took over as chairman or coordinator the survey course on humanities where I practiced the methods of cooperation and correlation to the utmost degree. I think that I have also shown, unconsciously, that different races and creeds can peacefully live together. The whole experience has been enriching and enlightening, for my colleagues (I hope) and for me.

Finally I wish to say that my contribution has been recognized in a way which seems to be rather embarrassing to me. I have come here as instructor and am now (at least during the absence of the chairman of my department) not only the acting head of my department but also of the entire division of Languages, Literatures and Fine Arts. And for three years I have been the chairman of the Language Group of the State Educators' Association. It is understood that I give only a general, true picture omitting those shortcomings which disturb American teachers and me (naturalized citizen) alike, as for instance the library problem in smaller colleges, far away from the great cities, and private problems that interfere sometimes when you need to concentrate on serious matters.

A scholar in the field of law makes this statement:

I find the American system of legal education, and particularly the case method of instruction, far superior to the system of education prevailing on the Continent. The main advantage of the American system lies in the fact that it makes for a much greater intellectual independence on the part of the student than the lecture method prevailing on the Continent. Furthermore, when I came to this country I was convinced that I understood the democratic way of life, but I realized pretty soon how much more genuinely democratic the system of education over here is as contrasted with the system prevailing even under the Weimar Republic.

Mingled praise and criticism are contained in this letter from the Middle West:

The overemphasis on administration and the concentration of power in hands of men who have little or no firsthand knowledge of creative scholarship is at times most annoying and very detrimental to the spirit of the academic staff and to creative work. In this respect, however, I do not think that I was the victim of any specific antiforeign feeling or any preconceived antiforeign policies. My rather sad experience on this score is shared by a great number of the faculty people, certainly the majority of the more active and younger men. . . . After becoming thoroughly acquainted with American universities I can only say that I am very greatly impressed by and thoroughly sold on the much more democratic educational policy exercised in this country as compared with Europe. The fact that students of very limited financial means have at least a good chance to acquire an academic education is the most pleasing, the most encouraging, and the most hopeful aspect of academic life here. It outweighs in my opinion already in its present form most if not all of the criticism which is frequently leveled against the universities in this country. I am sure that a further strengthening of the democratic system of education through state and federal fellowships represents one of the greatest hopes of the country. I sincerely hope that such fellowships will be made available on a very large scale.

An interesting statement comes from a professor in an urban institution:

By training, personal inclination, and professional experience prior to my stay in America, I am interested at least as much in research and writing as in teaching. Consequently, I have found and still do find a weekly teaching load of fifteen hours an excessive burden. During the past ten years I have actually managed to devote a considerable portion of my energies to research and writing. However, occasionally this has involved a conflict of loyalties and, in the long run, a great physical and psychic strain which, at times, curbed the pursuit of happiness. The excessive amount of teaching, as I see it, endangers the quality and originality of teaching. It does not stimulate time-consuming meditation and organic intellectual growth and rejuvenation, which cannot be rushed or mechanically measured. A teaching load of fifteen hours exposes the teacher to the ever present temptation of seeking release from pressure by turning into a stale *routinier*. Deeply aware of this threat of gradual deterioration making for diminishing returns, I have found that the fight for quality versus quantity entails considerable nervous strain.

The American college, as an institutional pattern of higher learning, seems to rest on an unorganic and ill digested mixture of high-school standards and techniques and university standards and techniques. Or, to be quite frank and more specific, my "happiness" has not been complete by virtue of the intellectual atmosphere created by many teachers and students who are inclined to carry a high-school mentality into their "advanced" work and, hence, fail to strive for humanized culture, as that term has been defined by Matthew Arnold. . . . Almost universally I have met with great warmth of feeling, tenderness of the heart, and sympathetic understanding.

A European scholar considers the administrative set-up of American universities:

The members of the faculty are my best friends. The harmony and personal relationship is something I never experienced before. The students are, as a rule, of better quality than those I met in Europe. I like to work with them, and enjoy their active cooperation. As to administration, I could not yet fully conform myself to the here prevailing authoritarian system of administration. In my home country, Austria, the professor is truly a member of the faculty, participating, in accordance with the rank he holds, in the self-administration of the university. Rector (president) and deans are elected by the faculties or their representatives on a year's term. These officers continue as active professors, and remain your colleagues and friends. While in this country the professor is—judging from the experience at my university—a hired teacher subject to the administration with a very limited voice in it; thus, teaching staff and administration constitute two very distinctive branches of the "universitas."

One professor views the scene philosophically:

There were a considerable number of individuals among the faculty and administration who went out of their way to make life and adaptation easy for me; on the other hand, I considered it part of my efforts to make the students feel that I was just another instructor and, I believe I succeeded in this.

Having spent almost thirteen years in this country and having observed how other individuals in similar circumstances adapted themselves or failed to do so, I should like to state that, in my opinion, the answer to your first two questions seemed in many cases to depend on the *desire* of the person to feel happy, which is an attribute of personality and widely independent of the external conditions. On the other hand, there is a hankering in many people to feel unhappy, especially in middle age and later, which prompts them into ambitions which are apt to be unfulfillable; one of these being in our cases the ambition to play a role of importance in administrative affairs or others, interfering with the customary procedures of the American college, or, finally, the ambition of being evalued according to one's own scale of values. But these are attitudes which appear to be common to a large section of the community of scholars and do not have much to do with national origin.

A scholar writes of the reception he received:

When I came to   College in 1940 my colleagues in the faculty accepted me at once as a member of the college community and made me feel "at home" in every respect. Within the   Department I was given the opportunity to do the work which suited best my intentions and abilities. Colleagues from other Departments offered me frequently the possibility of lecturing to their classes on problems of art which seemed to be relevant to their courses. That I was elected and appointed to some faculty committees seems to show furthermore the kind of disposition of my colleagues towards me. When my wife joined me in 1941 she was received by my colleagues like an old friend of theirs. It is now the third year that she is teaching here. The Administration was equally kind to me. After having taught for three years I was promoted to an assistant professorship. As far as the students are concerned, it was certainly a pleasure working with them and I felt that they responded fully to my teaching.

A young scholar writes candidly of his early experiences in this country:

When I arrived at the University I was not, strictly speaking, happy for a number of personal reasons; when I left, I was, and I think my experiences at the University were the primary reason for this change of my frame of mind. In the beginning a number of circumstances aggravated my depressed mood. I was transplanted in a new world in more than one way: from a European to an American, from a graduate to an undergraduate school, from one educational system to another with different aims and ideas and methods, and most of all from city life to life not in the country but on the campus, i.e., cut off from the rest of the world. The fact that my income was very small and that I had no clearly defined status hurt my self-esteem and created many objective difficulties; perhaps the greatest difficulty was the feeling that my placement at the college was a matter of charity, a feeling engendered by the fact that part of my salary was not coming from the college although the institution continued to pay also this part when this other source failed to fulfill its commitments. In fact, the late President of the University, who assumed the role of a most considerate and sympathetic host, noted this predicament of mine and increased my salary on his own initiative.

Another problem was that I could not, for a considerable time, correctly grasp the mentality of the students and had difficulty in finding the right approach to them. I talked over their head, and they did not respond. However, they were patient, cooperative, and did want to do their best. I began to establish contact with many of them outside the classroom and gradually found the right tone in the classroom. My colleagues in the department and from other departments gave me all the support I needed by establishing a very friendly contact, opened their house to me, took personal interest in me and my problems, and helped me to overcome all my difficulties. Many of them became personal friends of mine and have remained so up to this day. After a few months I was able to get the students interested and aroused, and I participated in courses of my colleagues as well to give them more the character of a seminar conducted on a more mature level.

What I contributed to the life and development of the students I can only guess from the indirect signs (and a few explicit indications) in farewell letters addressed to me on my departure.

These comments come from a southern Negro institution:

I was happy to work and live with American Negroes and found the faculty members, the administration, and the students extremely pleasant. I formed lasting friendships. . . . The faculty consisted of a group of fine scholars, many of them with an international background. The interest for true scholarship was encouraging, the understanding of minority problems proved comforting. . . . Needless to stress that there was not the slightest friction or misunderstanding because of "race, creed, or color."

The writer of the following, like some other foreign scholars, found small colleges difficult to understand:

Although we were very kindly received by some members of the faculty, we felt from the beginning that we did not quite fit into the framework of a conservative, provincial, small college which stresses religion and abstinence, teaching and conformity to "the powers that be" at the expense of scholarship and variety of interests, of cosmopolitanism and originality.

This thoughtful comment comes from a scholar in the East:

I have derived great satisfaction from my work as a teacher in all the institutions with which I have been associated. Though none of these are sufficiently endowed to offer full-time work and consequently a salary sufficient for a livelihood, the fees I have received for lectures are the maximum which these schools can afford to pay. My satisfaction therefore, has been rather of a moral nature.

I was given full freedom both in arranging the plan of my courses and in the interpretation of historical problems. I have enjoyed the full cooperation and friendliest attitude from all my colleagues. Most of all I have been impressed by the attitude of my students. In contrast to most European colleges and universities where the relationship between the professor and the students is characterized by the hierarchic attitude of the former, the American student's relationship to his teacher is marked by a spirit of democracy. The respect of the student for the teacher here in this country, doesn't imbue him with shyness, and he feels completely free in discussions in the classroom. That I never experienced any sarcasm on account of my shortcomings in English speech or foreign accent, I consider a result of the same democratic practice.

The discrepancy between my secular, more specifically, socialist, approach to Jewish history and contemporary Jewish problems and the theological philosophy of many Jewish institutions of higher learning, scholarly societies and institutions for publications, has been the cause of some discriminatory experiences which I particularly resent because some of these institutions claim absolute impartiality in their program and in their treatment of scholars and scholarly works. I should not generalize, and these disillusionments rather served to stress even more favorably in my memory the lack of any bias as well as the objectivity of those institutions which gave me the opportunity to lecture and to publish my studies. In sum, I have rather the happy feeling of having done my share in education and Jewish studies and having found recognition for my work.

A teacher of psychology offers this observation:

I should like to say that the response a scholar of foreign background receives in this country is markedly different from that which he would receive in Europe. From my knowledge specifically of German universities, an accent or incorrect usage of the language would preclude the possibility of the individual's becoming a member of the teaching staff. The only exception is in the case of teachers of foreign languages. This leads me to the conclusion that, barring such labor problems as the effect of immigration, there is a greater awareness among students and faculty in this country that science is international and exceeds group boundaries.

This lack of awareness in Europe, specifically in Germany, might have been a co-determining factor in the accentuation of Nazi ideology in German universities, and accordingly might be changed in the present and future by exchange professorships. If German students would be exposed to the teaching of scholars from foreign countries as guests of German universities, they might gain an understanding of the universality of scientific facts and problems and their independence of barriers of language, mores, and political lines of division.

A well known psychologist offers food for thought:

One of the points which impressed me most deeply was the coming face to face with a culture in which science is fundamentally seen as a servant to human beings rather than a superhuman entity which universities and institutes have to serve, as is to a large degree the case in Germany. At the same time I have been impressed by the relative lack of interest in the theoretical approach which around 1932 was quite apparent. If I may venture a general remark, I would say that the feeling for what theory means in science and what role it should play has developed quite favorably during the last decade in those areas of science with which I deal, in part probably as the result of the immigrating scholars. I personally am of the opinion that it would be dangerous for American culture and for a democratic and peaceful world if the basic attitude toward science as a servant to the practical goals should be altered. But I feel this danger thus far has been avoided.

I feel that the Institute of International Education has done a very distinct service to all concerned with remarkably few failures, and I feel that linking scholars from the different countries together can be a major contribution to the development of science and good intercultural relations.

A sociologist makes these comments:

I do think that I have rendered a service. I have been able to give the students vistas which native sons could not have given, and I have been able to contribute some to the understanding of other countries by both college and town people.

Both my wife and I are grateful that we have spent these first years in the U.S.A. not in one of the big cities but in a "Middletown" where we had to integrate ourselves into American society whether we liked it or not. As no other refugee is located here, and as the German-speaking people were Nazified and consequently not in our sphere of contacts, we were not deterred from thorough "Americanization" by contacts with people from "the old country." This has made life rather difficult at first, but it has made the assimilation and integration easier and more fundamental than it would have been possible otherwise.

May I close this letter with an expression of very sincere thanks for the great and vital service which your Emergency Committee has rendered to me and my family and to all those others whose names appear in your lists. The history of the Committee will doubtless mirror this, but it cannot reflect the amount of happiness which your actions have created and the part which it has played in helping so many families to get started in this country which most of them, I am sure, will now gratefully consider to be their new homeland. For my children it is *the* homeland. Thank you and your Committee for that.

A scholar on the east coast writes as follows:

Both the College authorities and the members of the Faculty were extremely kind and friendly to me. They helped and encouraged me in all possible ways in my work and showed a deep human interest in my personal affairs. They never let me feel that I am a foreigner. I received from the President, his Secretary and various members of the Faculty considerable help in bringing my family to the United States and in placing my children in excellent American schools. My son is now in the American Army. My family was received here in the same hospitable, friendly, and warm way as I was myself. During the illness and after the death of my wife I received proofs of such deep and sincere sympathy that I shall never forget it.

The qualities and the attitude of the students deserve special praise. They were and are—in general—very diligent, responsible, and honest (many of them very intelligent), showing independence of opinions, naturalness in behavior, but at the same time respect for their teachers. They were also very kind and indulgent when, at the beginning of my teaching, my poor English and my foreign accent certainly caused them some trouble.

This letter is from a displaced scholar who is a full professor at one of the southern universities:

I have been Professor of Biology at   for seven years. I found here not only a harbor and a new home but also the possibility to continue my work as a teacher and scientist. I got a well equipped laboratory and room to build up my Museum. The salary is sufficient for a modest living. I haven't been seriously ill during my stay here.

The members of the college faculty and administration were, in general, kind and helpful. I am especially grateful to the students. From the very beginning, at the time when my English was still poor, they were full of understanding and cooperation. In 1943 the student body dedicated the "Yearbook" to me. I quote the dedication, not in order to show off, but to demonstrate the charming attitude and appreciation of the students: "The students of   hold it a happy pleasure and deem it a high privilege to dedicate the yearbook of Nineteen hundred and forty-three to Dr.   in whom they recognize a scientist of wide renown—whose scholarship is one of brilliant attainment—whose noble qualities as a professor are such as become a great teacher—whose patriotism is like unto a pure white flame that knows no wavering—whose friendship is held dear and priced as a valued possession."

The answer about my service as a teacher is partly given by the dedication quoted above. During my stay here I built up the   Museum, which, I hope, will become an asset to American science.

In 1944 I and all members of my family became American citizens. Both my sons have been and still are overseas with the American Armies, the elder one now in Japan, the younger one with the Intelligence Service in Heidelberg, Germany. My wife has been an active member of the American Red Cross and of its Canteen Corps. Thus, I think that my family and I did a real service to my new country during the time of war.

I want to express again my deep appreciation and sincere gratitude to the Emergency Committee in Aid of Displaced Foreign Scholars. Without the quick and generous help by the Emergency Committee I wouldn't have been able to establish myself and my family so safely and quickly. If we were and, I hope, will be able to do a real service to our new country, it was made possible by the splendid assistance we received from the Emergency Committee. We shall never forget to remember it gratefully.

CHAPTER X

Opinions of College and University Administrators About the Displaced Scholars

AFTER the Emergency Committee completed its work in June, 1945, we sent a letter to the presidents of colleges and universities in which displaced scholars taught, part of which follows:

We are anxious to have an unbiased expression from you of the reaction of your institution to the presence of the displaced foreign scholars on your campus. I am wondering therefore whether you or the administrative officer most conversant with the scholars' work would be willing to answer the following questions. This is a great deal to ask of a busy administrator; I hope it may not appear too much.

1. Were the displaced scholars in your institution readily absorbed?
2. Did they provide a problem, and if so what was its nature?
3. Did they make a scholarly contribution to the institution, and if so of what kind?
4. Have you any general comments?

Please note that no names or identifying data will be used in connection with any excerpts which we may publish.

Cordially yours,

STEPHEN DUGGAN, *Chairman*

Emergency Committee in Aid of Displaced Foreign Scholars

Responses to this letter of inquiry were preponderantly favorable. A number of presidents and deans made the point that refugee scholars differed among themselves just as much as American professors did. An overwhelming majority emphasized the contributions, usually scholarly ones, which had been made by the refugee professors.

On the whole, college administrators tended to look back upon the introduction of displaced scholars as an outstanding benefit to American education. In the words of one university president, "The United States profited greatly by Hitler's mistakes"; and the sentiment of a well known president of a women's college was echoed by many: "I have no general comment except to say that, if the world ever gets caught in the same situation again, I hope arrangements will always be made for making room in academic communities for displaced members from other lands."

The authors were obliged to choose from among the scores of letters received since not all could be used. They have attempted in the pages which follow to present through typical excerpts a fair picture. In such slight editing as was done, changes were made in the wording only when paraphrasing was necessary in order to prevent identification of the scholar described or the institution reporting. Omissions within the text in all significant instances have been indicated. All proper names have been deleted.

An institution with a long liberal tradition states:

To answer your questions specifically and in order, I think it fair to say that the displaced scholars here have been readily absorbed. This is a liberal community and a hospitable one. With foreign-born members of the faculty, it seems natural to have "foreigners" coming to the faculty. The Quaker background together with the liberal academic atmosphere developed by President   combined to make the displaced scholars themselves feel reasonably at home and to make us accept able people as a matter of course.

Some of these displaced scholars are still on our faculty; the majority have moved on to other positions. So far as I know, those who have moved on have, as a result of their experience here, been in a position to command a better salary and permanent or semipermanent openings elsewhere. According to their ability, they have made both a scholarly and a pedagogical contribution to this College.

What has impressed me most is not the difficulty which the Germans in particular have in adapting their Teutonic background and experience to the American undergraduate scene—and it should be borne in mind that these men have been teaching in an undergraduate institute—but their success in making the adjustment. There is no question that the presence of these foreign scholars has enriched American education. It has provided a great diversity of points of view, and it has brought to us many men of distinction.

An eastern college reports:

The foreign scholars were readily absorbed in our institution. In spite of the peculiar nature of the small American residential college, the newcomers soon realized the difference between such institutions and the universities abroad. They made great efforts to adjust themselves to the life here and to the kind of teaching they were called upon to do. Naturally some were more flexible than others and made their way more quickly.

I know of no "problems."

As scholars and artists they have contributed through their publications and their performances. In some instances, furthermore, their attitude towards teaching was nearer to the principles on which the College's educational program is based than that of teachers whose habits were formed in the traditional American colleges. In spite of the prevalence of the lecture method in European universities, most of our newcomers were glad to give that method up for the tutorial and seminar methods. They treated our students as mature people who came to learn, and they found a genuine response. I mention this fact because it was an agreeable surprise to me.

My only general comment is that the country should be grateful for the wholehearted way in which most of the displaced scholars entered into the life of their adopted country. I feel that they have enriched the communities into which they have come.

From a famous college for women comes this statement:

I was greatly impressed with the evident effort made by these scholars, and others whom we appointed, to identify themselves with the college life. They were more regular in attendance on college affairs than our American faculty. They were exceedingly popular among the students.

One of the prized honors among the faculty is the dedication of the college annual of the senior class. This choice is made by free election and is absolutely without pressure. Two of our annuals in recent years have been dedicated to displaced scholars. This speaks for itself.

In several instances the wives of foreign scholars, themselves scholarly in their own right, have joined our faculty. They have never provided a particular problem. . . . These professors have made a genuinely scholarly contribution to the institution in their articles and studies, in their lectures, and in their contribution at faculty meetings.

There have been some criticisms of the European influence exerted by these scholars, who have, of course, brought with them certain predilections in favor of a somewhat stricter system of studies than prevails in our American college; but, on the whole, they have been accepted as full and unqualified members of our teaching staff with every privilege. In each case when one of these scholars has become an American citizen, the occasion has been celebrated with a friendly banquet and expressions of good will on the part of their colleagues.

A middle western institution which extended a warm welcome to refugees states:

Since 1939 we have entertained in the College seventeen displaced foreign scholars, most of them on appointments of one year or more. Five of these were French; ten were German or Austrian; and two were Italian. One of the former Germans, now an American citizen, is a lifetime member of the College faculty as a full professor. Most of the others took part in the Pre-Meteorology or the Area and Language training programs which the College undertook on behalf of the Air Corps and of the Army.

In answer to your questions:

1. They were readily absorbed into the institution.

2. Their problems were individual and peculiar to themselves as persons, and only in the slightest degree common to their status as displaced scholars. I have the impression that those who worked comfortably and easily with their colleagues in Europe did the same thing here, and those that probably produced friction abroad are the ones who in small ways became involved in little misunderstandings in the faculty. I should not think that those misunderstandings were proportionately more numerous among the displaced scholars than among any group of scholars.

3. They made a distinguished scholarly contribution, first of all, in the stir of discussion and traffic of ideas which they stimulated and promoted, and, in the second place, in the numerous articles and studies which they pursued and some of which they published while here.

There is no question that their presence was of great value and a stimulus to us. They brought to students a sense of university traditions other than our own, and a touch of the large world of scholarship and science, which was enhanced somewhat by the slight strangeness of the visitors. More than that, they illustrated the universality of learning to young men who without the experience of sitting under them would have had less notion of it than they obtained. There is no question that the immigration of scholars to this country brought to us something rare and valuable.

A municipal college has this to say:

Virtually all the displaced scholars appointed here adjusted themselves to our way of life rapidly and became effective educators in the American sense of the term. Some have become valued permanent members of the staff.

They did not provide a problem as a group. Their associations with one another did not result in bloc organizations and did not transcend the limits of what might normally be expected of intelligent people who had shared many experiences. Individually one or another of them had difficulties in adjusting himself to American teaching methods and to college teaching. One or two tended to look down upon American cultural and educational standards more than the situation really warranted. Some problems were entirely personal and in no way related to the status or the foreign background of the individuals. But without exception and with good success they strove to make the necessary adjustment.

Their scholarly contribution was noteworthy in all respects: in the enrichment of the classroom experiences of our students, in the stimulation of our curriculum through new ideas and approaches, and in the stimulation and enrichment of their colleagues in the profession as a whole by scholarly discussions, lectures, and a wealth of significant publications.

On the whole we are enthusiastic about this phase of Hitler's contribution to our educational and cultural welfare.

A university below the Mason-Dixon line reports:

We have had on our faculties some of these persons, and some of them are still with us as permanent members of our teaching staff. Others came only for a short term with aid put at their disposal through the University by friends who hoped that the scholars could earn a place for themselves either here or elsewhere. In general, my check shows that the men fitted in very well indeed, some of them especially well. The criticism from the Medical School concerned German and Austrian scholars; there it was found that from the standpoint of science they made a good showing. They did find it difficult to fit in personally as well as could be wished. Other scholars who are still with us have been for the most part entirely satisfactory. Of course in some instances inability to use the English language fluently and without foreign accent has been a deterrent, especially where students concerned were undergraduates.

From a large west-coast university comes an expression of confidence:

Your letter of November 9, inquiring as to the reaction of the University to the presence of displaced foreign scholars on this campus, evokes a very ready response. They have, indeed, been readily absorbed within the University in general. Of those who came to us, two have already gone to other institutions to carry on their work. The remainder, the very largest number, attained permanent rank at the University and have shown themselves to be able scholars and very satisfactory teachers. In general, they did not provide a problem; they sought to adjust themselves to the institution, and their colleagues found them men worth knowing and having in the faculty. They made their contribution through their broad and sound scholarship. Their interest touched numerous fields, and in this way their influence extended beyond their own particular field.

Brief comments taken from scattered letters show a warm appreciation of the scholars' contributions. This statement comes from Northern New England:

To my knowledge many fitted into their surroundings well and are still making a fine contribution. The venture seems to me to have been entirely worth while. As I kept in touch with it I felt that a number of new and important educational ideas were worked out.

This comes from the Middle West:

We consider the work of the Emergency Committee in Aid of Displaced Foreign Scholars one of the outstanding contributions to American education. The scholars appointed here were excellent men, who were readily absorbed into our life, who contributed much to our life and to scholarship generally, and who presented no special problem.

From a leading West Coast university came this praise:

These displaced scholars have not provided a problem for the University. Instead they are very valuable additions to our staff. Their scholarly contributions are outstanding in research as well as teaching. We are pleased indeed to have them as members of our faculty.

A university which had had two displaced foreign scholars on its faculty offered this comment:

Both men had some difficulty at first in the matter of language but after overcoming this obstacle, they were absorbed into our University family and community in a very fine manner. Both men are giving outstanding service as teachers.

A university in the South looked back pleasantly to its association with a displaced scientist:

We have had a professor who left Germany in 1937 or 1938 and who has subsequently taken out his citizenship papers. He has fitted in excellently and is, in fact, one of our most promising research men.

One college in a state notable for its concentration of educational institutions was able to report of a displaced scholar on its faculty,

He has made a scholarly contribution to the institution through his insistence on high standards of scholarship and the wide base he has tried to put under all of his teaching. When an inspector from the State Department of Education visited our institution, he said that the best teaching he saw while he was here was in Dr. B.'s classes. His teaching methods are good, and he gives himself to his teaching in a hearty way.

A university in the East states,

Our experience with the relatively few displaced scholars on this campus has been most satisfactory. Two men in the field of nuclear physics have recently been acclaimed through the country for their work on the atomic bomb project, although their distinction in research has been acknowledged by physicists for several years . . . All that I can think of have proved adaptable to the work of their departments, but they have varied in the extent to which they were absorbed socially in the community. I can think of no special problem that their presence created, and I know that as a group they have made an outstanding contribution.

A large Eastern institution reported in part as follows:

Of some 14 displaced scholars who came here, four became members of the faculties with tenure equivalent to that of their American colleagues. Of these, three were senior people of established reputation while one was a younger man of clearly marked brilliance. Those who did not remain were either personally and intellectually not adaptable to our conditions, or clearly temporary visitors who returned to Europe, or went to other American universities; or younger men for whom a temporary post was provided while they were trying to find permanent posts. The question of absorption could properly only be applied to about half of the total group. The absorption ratio is thus four out of seven.

The problem presented by the group as a whole was primarily to provide working arrangements and living expenses whereby they might continue their scholarly work. They were never considered as charity or relief problems. There was virtually no opposition to their entry into the university community, in fact most of them were invited by and supported for an initial period by the members of the faculties. Some personal problems of adjustment were encountered but in general these were of the same sort and frequency as might have accompanied the reception of a group of 14 Americans.

The most significant contributions in biochemistry to come from the university were made by one of this group . . . Several made smaller contributions to scholarly work while a few, by their lectures and contacts with students, aided in the educational work of the university. On the whole the chief contribution was to research and about in proportion to the numbers and length of tenure of the refugees. Most of them adjusted themselves quickly and continued their scholarly work.

There is little doubt that the net result was of benefit to the university and to the United States since the refugees nearly always added themselves to those groups within the university which have a primary devotion to pure scholarship and often brought to these groups the mature and catholic viewpoints of European scholarship.

Not all administrators, however, reported such favorable adjustments. A group of such judgments, from institutions representing widely scattered geographical areas, follows:

We had only one displaced foreign scholar during the period of the wartime emergency. This scholar was not well adapted to life at our institution, and we were unable to find a place for him following the termination of his initial contract. He did make some scholarly contribution in a group of articles which were published in learned journals.

While definite judgment must be based on each individual case, it is my opinion that the majority of foreign scholars brought to this country were not well adapted to the teaching of American undergraduates. Both language difficulties and the different procedures of American and European universities and colleges made it difficult for many of them to adjust themselves successfully to the demands of undergraduate instruction in this country.

From another university president:

1. "Were the displaced scholars in your institution readily absorbed?" On the whole, they were not readily absorbed. Considerable difficulty was encountered in assigning work to the displaced scholar on our campus. The two who were at the School of _____ were more readily assigned to classes which were available at that time. The three men were not readily absorbed by the departments or faculties concerned. However, they were with us for a very short time, and the problem of absorption was only a little greater in degree in their cases than for the average new faculty member.

2. "Did they provide a problem, and if so what was its nature?" All three did provide us with some problems. One exceedingly cultured individual was not at all familiar with the teaching methods which are successful in the United States; another individual was quite unstable emotionally, and this misfortune adversely affected his work in the classroom and his relations with his colleagues. Two of the men were primarily research scholars and unfamiliar with modern teaching methods. Their educa-

tional philosophy was in tune with the European university tradition and not suited to the less carefully selected and proportionately much larger student population of the American college and
university.

3. "Did they make a scholarly contribution to the institution,
and if so of what kind?" Some of these men made outstanding
contributions. One of them, in particular, published two or three
volumes in the field of economics, which received favorable re-
views nationally. Another one has written several articles of a
high order for learned journals dealing with the culture of   .
These men were trained in the traditions of research, and their
presence was a stimulation to our own faculty in that regard.

4. "General comments?" There are exceptions to all rules, of
course, but in general, the European scholar does not fit readily
into a teaching position in an American undergraduate institution. He is more at home on the graduate level, especially when
associated with research scholars. It would be helpful if men coming from abroad to teach in American institutions could be put
through a training course in some convenient place, possibly New
York, which would give them an understanding of the environment in which they are going to function and equip them to do
so successfully.

An administrator reported:

We have had only two, one of whom has made an extraordinary
contribution and is now a permanent member of our faculty.
The other has not worked out so well. He is having some difficulty being absorbed by the community because of certain fundamentally minor but annoying personality problems. Both of
these men are a real scholarly benefit.

Another President replied:

From my knowledge of the situation I find it difficult to make
generalizations that would apply to all those who served for a
time at this University either on special grants or through absorption into our regular budget, for our experiences with them have
varied greatly.

1. As a whole they did not fit too readily into our faculty or-

ganization, although there were a few conspicuous exceptions. In general the experiment was most successful with those who came for special research projects, and who thus worked individually and not as members of established departments of instruction. A few of them, however, gave such valuable service that they continued along with us.

2. In so far as there was a problem, it was only of personal adjustment. One or two of these scholars were rather arrogant in their attitude toward their colleagues. How far this was a personal shortcoming, and how far it might be accounted for by tragic, personal experiences, it is hard to say. I had experience with one, for example, who was glad to accept a temporary appointment for teaching with the understanding that it was for only one year to replace an absent member of the faculty, but later turned on me rather savagely when told that the appointment could not be continued indefinitely. One is apt to keep in mind the exceptions, however, and perhaps I ought to be thinking rather of another scholar who is still with us as a brilliant addition to our Department of   .

3. In general their scholarly contribution through research and —to a more limited extent—advanced teaching was significant.

4. All in all, we are grateful to the Emergency Committee for the opportunities it gave us. We are sure, too, that its activities meant much to scholars who through no fault of their own found their life-work seriously disturbed by being forced into exile.

An administrator in a large Middle West university writes:

We had a comparatively small number of these foreign scholars who actually came into our faculty. I do not think that we can say they were readily absorbed, for only one out of four became a member of the regular staff; furthermore, it cannot be denied that they presented a problem in the sense that they caused apprehension on the part of other staff members, especially the younger ones, as to their seniority in the department concerned. On the other hand, it cannot be denied that they made a scholarly contribution to the institution, bringing new viewpoints and a considerable amount of ability. I do not believe that we have any further comments to make on the matter in general.

A New England college reports:

As you of course realize, the questions are very difficult to answer because what is true of one displaced foreign scholar is not necessarily true of another.

1. "Were the displaced scholars in your institution readily absorbed?" In general, yes, but in varying degrees.

2. "Did they provide a problem, and if so what was its nature?" Nearly every one provided a problem of some sort naturally. The language was the most common problem but was by no means insurmountable, and the benefits derived from having the group here offset the difficulties. Some were, of course, suspected of anti-American activities, but so far as I know quite unjustly. A third problem concerned teaching methods in a few cases when the foreign scholar clung firmly to his own previous methods for rather too long a time. But in the end I think that every one has adapted himself. A fourth problem has concerned itself from time to time with the adjustment to the department in cases where administration rather than the department brought the scholar here, and it made a difficult situation for the chairman, either in regard to finance or fitting the scholar into departmental operations.

3. "Did they make a scholarly contribution to the institution, and if so of what kind?" Each one has made a scholarly contribution: some in writing and publishing; some in teaching; some because of their reputation outside the College.

4. "Have you any general comments?" In general, we have been very glad to have them here, and I think most of them have caused a minimum of difficulty and have added much to the spirit of internationalism. It has been an excellent thing from this standpoint for the students. Perhaps that has been the chief benefit. In individual cases mistakes may have been made which could have been avoided to some extent. However, in a first experience in dealing with such a situation there are bound to be ways which would bear improvement.

From a southern institution came the statement:

We have had several displaced foreign scholars, and we have found them to differ just as our own American scholars differ.

We have been so well satisfied with one of these men that he has remained with us and has been made Chairman of the Department. He is a scholar in every sense of the word.

Another person was something of a problem because she brought with her certain stereotype ideas with respect to authority and its place in academic life.

Another person was just a run-of-the-mine type, and he did not stay with us very long.

All in all, it has been our experience that some of these people are excellent, some of them are average, and some of them people who might not be able to remain on an American university faculty.

One president reported as follows:

1. Dr.   has been fairly readily absorbed.

2. The main problem in his case is one of personality. Fundamentally a kind, understanding, and devoted person and teacher of good standards, he remains somewhat insecure. This expresses itself in a certain overanxiety to make good in relations with his colleagues and with the administration. With students he is at greater ease and fully absorbed in his teaching. As a person he is not of immediately attractive appearance and voice; one grows to respect him on fuller acquaintance.

3. He contributes regularly to the scholarly journals in his field, applying his scholarly background to an analysis of contemporary economic situations and problems.

4. In the college he brings his background and convictions to bear in discussions within the social science faculty and in the faculty as a whole. His point of view is rather established than flexible. It contributes a certain diversity in our group.

An outstanding woman's college reported:

1. Within the limits of a) a very full program here which has consumed her time and limited wide associations within the group, b) a different approach to the teaching, and c) a somewhat retiring manner,   has been readily absorbed.

2. Other problems arose from her own distrust of her use of English, although never inadequate; her lack of acquaintance

with the life, attitudes, and problems of American girls; her concern for the destruction and disintegration in her own country with the recurring consideration of whether she could be more useful there. She has faced all of this with understanding and thoughtfulness and has made marked progress in establishing herself in her work.

3. She has done no writing. Her chief contribution is in discussion and planning within the faculty. She has been in considerable demand as a lecturer and participated in professional and international groups in the city.

4. She has been decidedly effective in the education of most of her students and is devoted to any work she undertakes.

Concerning one displaced scholar the report comes:

1. Dr.   is not as yet absorbed here, partly because of his limited assignment, but primarily because he is still finding his way into the most effective use of his materials and the appropriate methods in teaching college undergraduates. His position can be more fully evaluated as this year progresses.

2. The main problem is whether his own scholarly interests are too abstracted, and whether his own point of view is sufficiently integrated for effectiveness in teaching young students.

3. As yet there has been very limited opportunity for such contribution here.

4. He remains somewhat insecure since he has not found the status in this country which his attainments would appear to justify.

A careful statement from another institution made these points:

I have your letter asking for my impression of the adjustment which displaced foreign scholars have made on the campus. I believe that what I shall say represents the consensus of faculty opinion.

We have, I think, a very flexibly minded and cosmopolitan group of people here who are ready and eager to take to their bosom any person of real quality.   and   , for example, enjoy the affection of all of us; when Dr.   re-

cently accepted the chairmanship of the German Department at
another institution the expression of sorrow was universal and
heartfelt on our campus; the recent decision of   , an
exiled Spanish diplomat, to return to our faculty after his army
service is being hailed with delight.

The chief difficulty, apart from personality problems, in adjusting displaced scholars has been of course to get them to understand that the American college is neither Gymnasium (lycée,
liceo) on the one hand, nor a continental university on the other.
But once more, if they are not afflicted with arrogance, they
seem very quickly to understand the distinctive octave of values
within which we sing our song, and to join harmoniously in the
chorus. In retrospect, it will probably appear that the greatest
defect in our whole helter-skelter effort to find new homes for
displaced scholars was the lack of any effort to give them an
explicit understanding of what the American system of education is all about. If, for example, the Emergency Committee in
Aid of Displaced Foreign Scholars had issued a little pamphlet
for their indoctrination, much agony might have been saved.

As for the scholarly contribution of displaced academicians,
there can of course be no doubt. Of all the exiles now with us,
the one who leaps most immediately to mind is Dr.
formerly of Vienna, who next Tuesday is speaking to our faculty
research club. He is an absolutely first-rate Sinologist who handles
both Chinese and Russian, and is concerned with the influence
of the nomads upon the development of the Chinese civilization.
He publishes steadily and excellently, and lectures to large and
enthusiastic classes.

One suspects that Europe will continue to pass through grave
difficulties, and that no inconsiderable group of scholars will try
to reach this country within the next few years. I am glad that
you are working on the history of your committee because it may
be that from the experience of the crisis of the past twelve years
we can gain wisdom to meet similar problems during the next
decade or so.

Another college saw the situation thus:

This College did not make use of many displaced scholars as
regular members of the teaching staff. The faculty raised a fund

for the bringing of displaced scholars as visitors to the College. We had fourteen such visitors, one or two of them returning for second or third appointments. By and large, I should say that the project was extremely valuable. In view of the fact that we were not trying to absorb them as permanent colleagues, I hardly have enough data to answer your first question. Certainly as visitors they were a very fine addition, and in that role were absorbed with great appreciation. In several instances they provided very real problems as unhappy human beings for whom there was little professional future available. The complication of adapting a person from an entirely different educational system into a going concern was real and challenging. I suspect, however, that the ones who were strong in leadership at home were strong here, and that we had our fair share of people who would not have been particularly effective even in familiar surroundings. In other words, my impression was that the displaced scholars were as varied in ability as any cross-section of the faculty of American institutions.

Some of them made a scholarly contribution by challenging the assumptions of groups of students and by demonstrating that there is a universality of learning which made it possible for foreigners to be at home even in these strange surroundings.

I have no general comment except to say that, if the world ever gets caught in the same situation again, I hope arrangements will always be made for making room in academic communities for displaced members from other lands. It is my continuing impression that it is fair neither to the displaced scholar nor to the institution to assume that the visitor should be put at once into the regular teaching staff. While this would give him a certain sense of security, it puts a demand upon him which few of our visitors seem ready to meet. To ask a stranger to conform to all the practices of an American institution while he is making his own personal adjustment to a tragic upheaval is hardly fair. To waive those requirements puts him at a disadvantage with his colleagues. I have been glad, therefore, that we were able to entertain so many people as visitors; and I think our relationship with foreign colleagues is better than it would have been if we had tried to employ rather than to entertain them. As a matter of fact, two of our visitors are now with us on the faculty.

Thoughtful and considered was this statement:

It is my opinion that Dr.   fitted as well into our
faculty as could be expected of a person in his circumstances.
Despite the most cooperative sort of attitude on his part it has
not been easy in all cases to fit him into the regular work of the
School. Students at times object to his accent, a fact that was
particularly noticeable during the war years, and on occasion he
is inclined to expect special treatment.

In terms of the regular work of the School of   it is
probable that for a similar expenditure of money the School
could have employed a more competent instructor; but, in general, the experience of the School with Dr.   has been
reasonably satisfactory, and we have been happy to make this
contribution toward the program of absorbing men who, through
no fault of their own, were forced to find places for themselves
as a result of the situation which developed in Germany.

Typical of several frank evaluations was the following:

I have your inquiry with reference to displaced foreign scholars.
For two years we had on our faculty a German émigré, and I
shall give you my candid reactions concerning him, although I
am not certain that he has even been under the auspices of your
Committee.

Dr. X, as we shall call him, proved to be a congenial, middle-
aged man, of considerable erudition in a number of fields. He
was readily accepted by the faculty and made a number of warm
friends on the faculty. He was so ineffective as an undergraduate
teacher, however, that we finally had to let him go. Although he
was very cooperative in manner, the various suggestions made to
him from time to time concerning his work seemed to have no
particular effect. He was not essentially a "difficult person" but
made no particular effort to adjust himself to the local situation,
and I imagine behaved very much the same way here as he would
have anywhere else. If he had been a member of a department of
eight or ten people we might have been able to keep him on in
a highly specialized role, but he was a member of a department
of three persons and simply could not swing his part of the gen-

eralized undergraduate load. Dr. X. came to us with a distinguished publication record and, I presume, continued to publish in his own specialized field. Three or four people on a faculty of eight found him to be very stimulating in a scholarly way, but he was such a recluse that he made very little impression one way or the other on the majority of our faculty.

I respected him as a gentleman and a scholar and at the same time felt rather sorry for him—realizing that in some respects he was too good for us and in other respects not good enough. Like a number of other émigrés he belongs in a highly specialized post in a major university, but he is really not outstanding enough to meet the competition he would encounter. I suspect that his plight is the plight of other middle-aged émigré scholars who will never succeed in rooting themselves very firmly on an American college or university campus where undergraduate teaching is a prime function.

Another administrator wrote in similar vein:

In answer to your letter of November 9, may I say that we have had two refugee scholars on our campus. I must admit to you that both of these men have only been fairly satisfactory, so far as integrating themselves into our work here is concerned. This, of course, is no reflection on their scholarship; but in the very nature of the case our small school (limited to an enrollment of five hundred) is somewhat like a family experience, or at least in many ways it is so. In a situation, for example, where such men as we have had could simply go to their classrooms and teach their subjects and then be free from other obligations, they might make a very significant contribution. But when, in a situation like ours, it is necessary to be counselors with students and to meet with them in social ways and in religious meetings, and so on, it seems very difficult for these men to make the adjustment necessary to become readily absorbed and integrated into our situation. While our students have been impressed with the scholarship of these men, on the whole it has been difficult for them to communicate their learning to the students.

The following statement comes from an urban college in the East:

We have on our staff three men who should probably be considered displaced foreign scholars, though only one of them answers without question to that appellation.

All three were readily absorbed and have contributed to the work of the college by their continued scholarship, as well as by their popularity in the classroom and their general adaptability.

Perhaps we have been unusually fortunate in the individuals who came to us; but, to my mind, a native-born instructional staff can profit greatly from some admixture of scholars trained in other countries.

The administrative officer of a technological institute in the East declares:

In response to your inquiry of November 9, careful inquiry among the members of the Faculty fails to elicit any indication that a problem of any sort was created in this institution by the presence of displaced foreign scholars; in fact the response from one professor was, "They were absolutely swell."

I do not find a record of any particular contribution to the institution from these scholars, but the general reaction seems to be that we were glad to have them with us for a time.

A church-related university reports its experience:

In answer to your questions regarding displaced foreign scholars, I am very glad to say that they were readily absorbed into our organization and presented no problems. It may be that our policy in dealing with these men had something to do with the success of the venture. We made it a rule to give them temporary appointments which enabled us to size them up, so to speak, before admitting them to regular status on the staff. This worked very well. All told, we have had nine of these scholars, six of whom now have the rank of full professor; one holds the rank of visiting professor; and one is an assistant professor.

A college in the interior states:

1. We employed for a period of one year one displaced foreign scholar. He was most readily and satisfactorily absorbed in the work and life of the college.

2. No problem of consequence was encountered. At the beginning of his stay on the campus, there was some little difficulty with the language problem but a satisfactory adjustment was made without serious difficulty.

3. In my mind, the principal contribution of this staff member was in bringing to our students a wealth and richness of experience which could not be obtained in any other way. His social, intellectual, and political background was such that he was able to introduce the students to a world that otherwise would have remained closed to them. Also, his approach to the methods and procedures of teaching, based as it was on his experiences, was most stimulating to our students.

4. My only comment in connection with the work of this staff member was that it was in every way a continually satisfactory experience.

A large eastern university writes:

For the most part the displaced foreign scholars who came here came not as members of our faculties but as research fellows on brief appointment in the different schools and departments. With regard to this group I think I can say without qualification that they all proved to be quite at home in our laboratories and that their research work while here was creditable both to themselves and to the University.

With regard to the smaller group who came to positions on our faculty, the appointments in most cases were for limited duration, and these individuals have now left the University. I cannot say that all individuals in this group proved to be easily absorbed into the activities of the University. The difficulties on this score, when they arose, were due either to the individual's lack of acquaintance with the teaching methods of American universities or to his disappointment when the University found that it was unable to continue his assignment on our faculty indefinitely. I do not wish to emphasize the difficulties unreasonably, for they were in all cases of no great moment and appeared only with regard to a very few people.

For the most part our visiting professors in this group proved to be both welcome and respected members of our departmental faculties. Their success here was due to the fact that they brought a new and refreshing point of view to bear upon the subject matter of the classroom and were as well scholars of distinction whose interests in investigation provided a stimulus for the younger members of our own faculty.

If I should add a statement by way of general comment it would be to the effect that this institution has benefited on the whole from its experience with displaced foreign scholars and appreciates the activities of the Emergency Committee which enabled the University to bring these people to us.

The following excerpt is taken from the letter of an administrator of a southern university:

We have had at the University only two of these scholars. One remained for about three years and then accepted a position elsewhere. One of the men is still with us.

Both of the displaced scholars whom we brought to the University fitted extremely well into the University community. Both of them are gentlemen and scholars in every sense of the word. They made a splendid contribution to the work of the institution particularly in the classrooms, in scholarly writing, and in general contact with members of the faculty and of the University community.

A coeducational institution reports:

With one exception these men were not problem cases. The one exception we should have been glad to see called to another institution. No calls have developed, and we are carrying him on an inadequate stipend because if we dropped him from our rolls he would be on the street.

One of the group proved such a stimulating influence in his department that he was elected to a full professorship and has become recognized by his colleagues as one of the most valuable members of the department. I think the group as a whole (which, of course, was not large) more than pulled its weight in the boat.

This comment comes from an institution in New York State:

This University had no difficulty in absorbing the scholars who came to it. I believe in each case the Committee's nominee made quick and satisfactory contacts with all colleagues, socially as well as academically.

The only problem which the presence of these gentlemen raised came from their imperfect command of the English language.

The scholarly output of the gentlemen sent us by the Emergency Committee has been distinguished. Their productivity has been a stimulus to their departmental colleagues.

My only general comment is that the work of the Emergency Committee not only contributed to the intellectual and spiritual salvation of an extraordinarily gifted group of scholars, but also enriched the scholarly life of a great number of American institutions.

The following statement occurs in a letter from an institution in a large eastern city:

I am pleased to write this letter concerning the displaced foreign scholar who is now a full-time member of our staff. His excellent training and experience in Germany, his deep desire to become a citizen of the United States, and our need for one of his abilities in the School of Fine Arts made him a very happy member of our University family.

Until last Thursday, when he was naturalized, he was a citizen without a country. I attended a naturalization party at his home Saturday evening. He has a delightful family, is considered by his colleagues a scholarly member of the staff, and in so far as we are concerned will be permanently assigned to our staff in September, 1946.

A midwestern university reports:

The number of scholars here was so few that there was no problem in absorbing them. They were readily accepted, and, so far as I am aware, there was never any discrimination or any feeling that the displaced scholars themselves were displacing others who might have filled positions here.

One of the scholars, a chemist, at once made a name for himself and within a period of a few months was hired away from the University for an industrial position. Another, and the one who was longest with us, definitely stimulated an interest in the field of business cycles which was his own specialty. In fact, it was his energy that led to the establishment of a monograph series in business cycle theory. I think only one number was published, but nevertheless the impact of this man was evident.

I am confident that I summarize the general attitude of the faculty here when I say that in limited numbers foreign scholars were and can be absorbed into a university community.

An eastern university records its experience:

has appointed to its faculty a relatively small number of displaced scholars. It has been our policy to make such an appointment only when the man in question was a scholar of clear eminence. We have not appointed displaced scholars because we were sorry for them, nor because we could get them at a financial bargain.

In fear that the foregoing may seem to indicate that we followed a somewhat heartless policy, I should say that so far as we were concerned it seemed to be really in the best interests of the displaced scholar as well as of the University. Had we adopted any other we should not have succeeded, I fear, in maintaining an academic climate favorable to the scholar from abroad. We did receive some financial assistance from outside to apply to salaries, but in each case the outside grant was supplemented by our own funds to bring the salary within our normal brackets.

The problems of adjustment and absorption have in no case been serious—no greater than is usually the case when a foreigner undertakes to learn American ways. None of our displaced-scholar appointments has turned out to be a serious mistake. Several of them have made important contributions to the scholarly strength of our faculty.

From an institution in the Middle West comes this statement:

I am glad to be able to give you the following information regarding the displaced foreign scholars who came to University:

1. They were easily absorbed in the life and activities of the University.

2. They did not provide any special problem.

3. Their contributions to this institution were, in general, very much above the average.

4. My own contacts with displaced scholars, not only at   but at other institutions, lead me to feel that the United States profited greatly by Hitler's mistakes.

A northern college sends the following comment:

We had three displaced foreign scholars here who were more or less aided through your Committee. All three of these men were victims of the Hitler persecution and came through Austria. One was a learned scholar whom we would have gladly kept with us, but who was obliged to leave. The second man, a Czechoslovak with a charming Austrian wife, was a Ph.D. in Economics and Social Sciences. After about two years with us he received a better offering in a larger western institution where he is engaged in his chosen field of work. The third man, a native of Vienna, is an M.D. and a noted pianist and composer. He is still with us. All of these men gave every indication that they were very happy here and they soon overcame the handicap of the language and became very valuable members of our faculty. I may say that the other members of our faculty accepted them graciously, and so far as I could determine there was not the slightest mark of professional jealousy on the part of our own regular faculty.

As you know, this college is one of the smaller colleges. Yet despite the very great loss in students to the armed services our college kept going. I believe that, had it not been for some of the help received from your Committee, we would not have accepted the scholars mentioned above. There is no question in my mind that these men added greatly to the prestige of   and I agree with my friends of   that the College itself because of the times deserves equal credit by accepting these men.

Since my experience in this matter has been very limited, I fear that whatever general comment I could make would be of little value. There is, of course, a great deal of careless talking going around, but I cannot truthfully say that I have noticed any indication of professional jealousy among the members of our lay faculty. You have undoubtedly heard comments about the number of M.D.'s who have taken up practice in this country or are on the faculties of some of our medical colleges. I believe that we may have to face the fact that American scholars who gave themselves or who were in many cases taken into the armed forces will be displeased to find foreign scholars taking their places.

A church-related institution tells of a sucessful program:

Our experience with displaced scholars is too limited to be a basis for conclusions. We have not had more than eight. Of these, six were readily absorbed; none furnished any real problems. Six have added considerable distinction to the faculty.

Two further responses from colleges and universities in which displaced scholars taught, both of them from institutions in the middle western states, must suffice to complete the mosaic of judgments which have made up the material of this chapter:

Thank you very much for giving me an opportunity to convey to the Institute of International Education the appreciation of College for sending us a "displaced scholar."
He is not only a competent scholar, but also a gentleman in every respect. He has been most loyal to the institution and to the administration. All of us esteem him highly. We would consider it an irreparable loss to have him moved from our staff.

———

I should say that   College had had a very happy experience indeed with these scholars, and that they have brought a distinct enrichment to the life of the college. All were persons of distinction in their fields, and all except one maintain a thoroughly pleasant relationship with colleagues. Even in this instance one might say that during most of the time the relationship was a pleasant and constructive one. The students were enthusiastic about the work which was offered by each of the scholars— less so in the case of one, but in this instance the adjustment was better at the end of the period than at the beginning of the term here.

Two of the scholars provided absolutely no problem in any respect. Two have found difficulty in adjusting their language teaching to the methods used in an American college, but both made great strides during their period of service here.

I should say that every one of the group made a distinctly scholarly contribution to the college. As I think back over the group I believe that the greatest single contribution was their ability to cut across narrow fields of specialization. Each of them seemed to feel at home in a much wider area of knowledge and to see more clearly the relationships between the different fields than is sometimes true of American scholars.

Visiting scholars and students from other lands tend to make a group of American college students more cosmopolitan in their thinking and better prepared to understand the world responsibilities which their country will have in years just ahead.

CHAPTER XI

Origin, Organization, and Policies of the Emergency Committee

THE close of Chapter I mentioned the formation, early in May, 1933, of an organizing committee consisting of Dr. Cohn, Mr. Flexner, Mr. Stein and Dr. Duggan, which adopted the name Emergency Committee in Aid of Displaced German Scholars. The Committee proceeded vigorously to work. The following letter explaining the objective of the Committee was sent to the presidents of colleges and universities:

INSTITUTE OF INTERNATIONAL EDUCATION
2 West 45th Street, New York City

May 27, 1933

My dear President   :

A group of persons interested in the problem of the university professors ousted from their chairs in Germany because of their political opinions or race, has been holding conferences in New York to determine whether assistance might be granted by us over here, and the nature of such assistance. Several meetings have been held, and I have been requested to write to you concerning some of the plans that we have in view.

It is obvious that, because of the financial condition of our own institutions of higher education, they ought not to be called upon in any way for financial assistance. It would naturally cause resentment in our own country were moneys to be voted by universities for this purpose when so many of our own young instructors and assistant professors have been dropped from the rolls and are in dire need themselves. The funds necessary to carry out any program must be raised from sources outside the universities.

Individuals have already contributed some funds for this purpose, and this is also true of two foundations. If one of the great universities were to write to the group, stating that it would like to invite Professor "X" from among the ousted scholars to engage in graduate work, but that it had not the funds wherewith to do this, the group would meet the need to the extent permitted by the resources at its disposal. The group believes that the younger men ousted from the universities of Germany might be assisted to continue their work in the universities of European countries with aid furnished by the foundations. This would be less expensive and probably more helpful.

The Provisional Committee's view as to what ought to be done is as follows: A committee should be formed consisting, among others, of representatives of the Association of American Universities, the National Research Council, the Social Science Research Council, and the American Council of Learned Societies (representing the humanistic branches). To this committee a university should write, naming the distinguished authority in a specific field whom the university would care to invite. If it has no particular scholar in mind, the committee would be prepared to send a list of such men and women, from among whom a choice may be made. The Committee would provide the salary of the scholar invited. While the committee would like to have such a scholar receive as high a salary as the American professor, it thinks that, considering the matter is one of emergency, it should be less. Moreover, in order to avoid any resentment arising in educational circles in our own country from the belief that the foreign professor might remain permanently and occupy a chair in the university which an excellent American scholar might reasonably have looked forward to filling, the committee believes that the chairs that are to be filled should be honorary chairs, and that the invitation should be for a specific number of years— probably three—and that it should be clearly understood that any commitment on the part of the university itself or of the committee should stop at the close of that period.

I have personally talked this matter over with committees from Princeton and Columbia and with presidents of universities in different parts of the United States. There is general agreement as to the need of a committee representing the cultural interests of the country, to which the plan outlined above by the provisional committee may be submitted, and which will direct the realization of the program indicated. I am now, however, writing to the heads of our most representative universities to ask

1. Whether the provisional Committee may have the benefit of your criticism of the plan.

2. Whether your institution will participate to the extent and under the conditions indicated in the plan.

As the scholastic year is drawing to a close and the Committee would like to act as quickly as possible, I shall be much indebted for as prompt an answer as your engagements will permit.

Sincerely yours,
STEPHEN DUGGAN

P.S. The Committee requests that this information be restricted to university circles.

S.D.

It is a tribute to the broad-mindedness of our university men, and to their understanding of the crisis that had arisen in the domain of scholarship, that the letters of acceptance were nearly always accompanied by expressions of great satisfaction that the Provisional Committee had been organized, of hope that it would start its activities at once, and of a desire personally to do whatever was within the power of the writer to make the work of the Committee a success.

The following letter was then sent to distinguished scholars and university presidents inviting them to become members of the General Committee:

INSTITUTE OF INTERNATIONAL EDUCATION
2 West 45th Street, New York City

June 10, 1933

My dear President   :

You have already received a copy of the letter sent out by the Provisional Committee in Aid of Displaced German Scholars. The replies to these letters from the Presidents who have already answered are all favorable to the plan, only one hesitating to agree and then for another reason than disapproval.

The Provisional Committee wishes to have a General Committee made up entirely of university representatives. It does not want a committee of large dimensions, but it does want a committee that is representative of the scholarship and interest in international relations of our institutions of higher education. I am enclosing the list of those to whom requests are being sent. Some of these have answered the first letter so cordially—in some cases enthusiastically—that I believe they would not hesitate to permit their names to be used. If it will be agreeable to the membership of the General Committee, the officers of the Provisional Committee will be glad to continue to serve in the same capacities. They are: Livingston Farrand, Chairman; Stephen Duggan, Secretary; and Fred M. Stein, Treasurer.

Let me hasten to say that what is desired is a Committee whose standing in the world of scholarship and university affiliations will help to make the activity appear to the public to be one worthy of approval. The members will not be expected to meet and work; an Executive Committee will do that. Moreover, the safeguards provided in the plan which you have already received, for the rights of unemployed American teachers, for the temporary nature of the invitation to the German scholars, for the complete disappearance of any commitments on the part either of this Committee or of the University when the period of invitation comes to an end—these safeguards will be faithfully observed. The Provisional Committee wishes those invited to serve on the General Committee to understand that no new commitments of any kind, other than those outlined in the original plan, will be undertaken without everyone being consulted.

While we appreciate that there may be reasons why a scholar

or President invited to serve may not see his way clear to do so, we sincerely hope that the answers will be in the affirmative. We shall, moreover, appreciate as prompt a reply as your engagements permit.

Sincerely yours,

STEPHEN DUGGAN

Again the replies were of a nature to hearten the Committee in its work. They uniformly expressed belief in the need and importance of the plan and a desire to cooperate. Many educators consented to serve on the General Committee, which ultimately consisted of the following persons:

*Thomas S. Baker, Carnegie Institute of Technology
*Lotus D. Coffman, University of Minnesota
*Sir Arthur Currie, McGill University
  Harold Willis Dodds, Princeton University
  Sidney B. Fay, Harvard University
  Abraham Flexner, Institute for Advanced Study
*Harry A. Garfield, Williams College
  Robert M. Hutchins, University of Chicago
*James H. Kirkland, Vanderbilt University
  Henry N. MacCracken, Vassar College
  Robert A. Millikan, California Institute of Technology
  Wesley C. Mitchell, Columbia University
  Harold G. Moulton, Brookings Institution
*William A. Neilson, Smith College
*George Norlin, University of Colorado
  Marion Edwards Park, Bryn Mawr College
  Walter Dill Scott, Northwestern University
  Harlow Shapley, Harvard University
  Robert G. Sproul, University of California
  Oswald Veblen, Institute for Advanced Study
  Ray Lyman Wilbur, Stanford University
  Ernest H. Wilkins, Oberlin College
*Mary E. Woolley, Mount Holyoke College

---

* Now deceased.

Dr. Livingston Farrand, President of Cornell University, became Chairman of the Committee, Dr. Stephen Duggan its Secretary, and Mr. Fred M. Stein its Treasurer. Edward R. Murrow, the Assistant Director of the Institute of International Education, was asked to serve as Assistant Secretary, which he did until 1935, when he joined the Columbia Broadcasting System to become Chief of the European staff. It would be difficult to overemphasize the loyalty to the cause, the steadfast devotion to the work, and the efficiency of the results of Mr. Murrow's activities. When he retired from the Committee, Professor John Whyte, who was afterward Chairman of the Department of German in Brooklyn College, became the Assistant Secretary. His professorial duties, however, became so heavy that to the regret of the Committee he was compelled to resign in November, 1937. He was succeeded by Miss Betty Drury. Professor Nelson P. Mead of the College of the City of New York and Professor L. C. Dunn of Columbia University were added to Messrs. Cohn, Farrand, Flexner, Stein, and Duggan to form an Executive Committee.

In November, 1937, the Committee welcomed Charles J. Liebman, then Vice President and later President of the Refugee Economic Corporation, as a member of its Executive Committee. With him the Committee worked out plans for participating in the placement of displaced European scholars in Venezuela and the Philippines. As mentioned earlier, the Executive Committee had the good fortune in 1940 to add to its membership Dr. Frank Aydelotte of the Institute for Advanced Study, Dr. Hertha Kraus of the American Friends Service Committee, Dr. Alvin Johnson of the New School for Social Research, Dr. Henry Allen Moe of the Guggenheim Foundation and of the Oberlaender Trust, Charles A. Riegelman of the National Refugee Service, and Professor Harlow Shapley of Harvard University.

The Executive Committee held stated meetings every month except in summer. All the members of the Executive Committee were devoted to the work of the Emergency Committee, but it is not invidious to mention that without the unceasing efforts of Messrs. Stein and Flexner in interesting Jewish foundations to support this cause, the Emergency Committee could not have accomplished the great work that was done. The authors of this little volume cannot emphasize too strongly their admiration for the steadfast loyalty of these two men. The time, thought, and effort they gave to the work of the Emergency Committee appeared to have no limits. They were the driving force in its activities.

The Committee cannot adequately thank Miss Marie White, Mr. Stein's personal secretary, who kept its books during twelve active years. Miss White unselfishly contributed many hours of her own time year after year to the Committee's work.

In October, 1944, Miss Drury, who since 1933 had conducted the detail of the Committee's work, left the Emergency Committee to join the research staff of the Committee for the Study of Recent Immigration from Europe. The Committee was most fortunate in securing Mrs. Frances Fenton Park, formerly Dean of Smith College, to succeed her. Mrs. Park rendered unusual service in the closing period of the Committee's existence, after which Miss Drury returned to serve in a voluntary capacity as the Committee's Executive Secretary, carrying on its residual correspondence.

The name Emergency Committee in Aid of Displaced German Scholars was adopted because it was expected that the evil situation within Germany was an "emergency" or temporary one, which would change, even if only gradually. Few people anticipated that it would last twelve years and would extend through Central and most of Western Europe as the result of the Nazi conquests. This forlorn hope is well portrayed in a letter from an experienced observer within a year of the advent of Nazis to power:

In this matter of taking care of deposed scholars, one thought should be kept in mind; namely, that while the present Nazi regime will likely continue for some years at least, its anti-Semitic policy may well be modified within a few months. And since normally conditions for scientific work are better in Germany than in any country of Continental Europe, the ultimate return of a considerable number of the best of the deposed men—young and old—should be considered a probability. I therefore feel that it would be wiser to help establish these men in *temporary posts* than to cooperate in the establishment of permanent places, except of course where a return to Germany can be very definitely excluded. I talked to several Jews in London, including   , who felt that in the interest of the race the best men should stay in Germany, if possible, though they recognize that some scientists have been so deeply outraged that one should not expect them to stay on or go back for the sake of the race.

In addition to the letter sent to the presidents of colleges and universities, it was decided to request the learned societies to issue a statement of protest against the suppression of freedom of teaching in the German universities and persecution of professors because of reasons that had nothing to do with scholarship. The request was in the form of a letter sent by the Secretary of the Emergency Committee to the following officials of the learned societies:

Dixon Ryan Fox, American Historical Association
Virginia C. Gildersleeve, American Association of University Women
Robert Lincoln Kelly, Association of American Colleges
Charles B. Lipman, Association of American Universities
Ernest M. Patterson, American Academy of Political and Social Science
Edwin R. A. Seligman, American Economic Association
James T. Shotwell, American National Committee of International Commission on Intellectual Cooperation

H. W. Tyler, American Association of University Professors

Henry B. Ward, American Association for the Advancement of Science

The letter, dated December 16, 1933, was as follows:

H. W. Tyler, General Secretary
American Association of University Professors
744 Jackson Place
Washington, D.C.

My dear Professor Tyler:

I am enclosing a declaration concerning the suppression of freedom of speech and of teaching in Germany as a mere contribution to the subject. I am hoping that the great cultural organizations which usually hold their meetings during the Christmas holidays or in January will not let the occasion pass without taking some action on this question. I personally think we have reached a crisis in the history of human thought and its expression. I really believe that if we in the United States take action in the matter it will have a real effect in Europe, especially if the declaration is without political attachments—as this is.

I am not vain enough to suppose this is the right form of declaration, but it might suffice as a beginning for purposes of discussion. Were the associations whose names are given all to agree upon the same statement, and were teachers in our institutions of higher education to sign it in large numbers (I believe five thousand would gladly do so), I feel sure that the enemies of freedom of speech and of teaching would pause in their activity.

Unfortunately I sail tonight for Europe, to be away for some months, or I should personally follow up the attempt to get action upon the subject. I am hoping that if action is eventually taken, I may be permitted to be identified with it—even though I be absent—for I feel deeply upon the subject.

Sincerely yours,

STEPHEN DUGGAN, *Chairman*

*Committee on International Relations of
the American Association of University Professors*

The following Protest was drawn up by the Council of the American Association of University Professors, which represented twelve thousand professors in more than four hundred institutions of higher education throughout the country:

Protest Against Tyranny in German Universities

The American Association of University Professors is deeply concerned with the maintenance of those fundamental principles of academic freedom and tenure, without which university work of the highest quality cannot be permanently sustained.

The Council of the Association has become reluctantly convinced that in certain European countries and notably in Germany, so long and so honorably distinguished for its particular emphasis on *Lehrfreiheit* and *Lernfreiheit*, those high principles have been sacrificed and subordinated to political and other considerations ulterior if not irrevelant to true scientific research and scholarship.

The Council has no wish to express any opinion on the political life or ideals of any nation, but science and scholarship have long since become international, and the conditions of intellectual life in every important country are a matter of legitimate concern to every other. It is, therefore, resolved that this expression of the conviction of the Council and of its profound sympathy for members of the profession who have been subjected to intolerant treatment in these difficult times be published in the Bulletin of the Association and communicated to the Commission of Intellectual Cooperation of the League of Nations.

Though the International Commission of Intellectual Cooperation of the League of Nations had been formed to develop understanding and good will among the nations by means of educational and cultural agencies, no action was taken as the result of this communication. No protest was made to the German government and communicated to the governments of the other members of the League. The situation was ignored as far as the League of Nations was concerned.

The general belief that the evil events in German universities were only of a temporary nature and would soon be overcome was again made evident in the comment on the action of the Association by its President:

Evidence which seems conclusive has led the Council of the Association to the conclusion that a wave of emotion, without doubt caused by the recent distressing economic conditions under which Germany has been living, has brought about an unthinking, and, it is hoped and believed, temporary abandonment of the cherished principles of freedom of teaching and research. The resolution of the Council is published in the hope that it may aid those elements in Germany who seek a return to these well-tried principles of university organization.

The Emergency Committee wishes to record here its indebtedness to Professor H. W. Tyler, who was at that time the General Secretary of the American Association of University Professors, and to Dr. Ralph E. Himstead, who succeeded Professor Tyler upon the latter's death February 3, 1938. Both men were deeply interested in the work of the Emergency Committee and gave frequent help in solving its problems. The Emergency Committee wishes to express its indebtedness also to D. W. MacCormack (since deceased), the Commissioner of Immigration and Naturalization in the Department of Labor, for his helpful attitude in easing the immigration procedure for the incoming refugee scholars. The desire to serve in this cause was general throughout the country.

Once the colleges and universities had been informed of the nature of the Committee's program and its activities became known to displaced scholars, its work was greatly increased and accelerated. Difficulties of administration had already appeared in the United States and in England. For example, an excellent service organization, the National Coordinating Committee (later the National Refugee Service) had circularized the colleges and universities with requests for the appointment of refugee German scholars. As will be indicated later, such a procedure of soliciting jobs for refugees was in opposition to that adopted by the Emergency Committee. As the result of a conference between representatives of the two organizations it was decided that the National Coordinating Committee would no longer consider the placement of refugee scholars as part of its activities.

A similar situation had arisen in England. The Academic Assistance Council (later the Society for the Protection of Science and Learning) was quite overwhelmed by the numbers of displaced scholars who had fled to England seeking positions, and it was naturally inclined to seek assistance for the displaced scholars in the United States. As the Council was unfamiliar with the needs of our institutions and their methods of administration, this sometimes led to confusion of effort. E. W. Bagster-Collins, Professor of German at Teachers College, Columbia University, was engaged by the Emergency Committee in 1933 as its foreign representative. He went first to London to develop relationships with the Academic Assistance Council. He was requested by the Emergency Committee to make frequent trips to Germany for first-hand information about the dismissal of eminent German scholars, their whereabouts and availability for invitations to American institutions, and to deliver such invitations in person if necessary. It was early realized that extreme care would have to be used in communicating with the dismissed professors, and the Committee urged that where letters had to be written no allusion be made to the exigencies of the situation within Germany, and no mention be made of solicitations from the scholar himself for help in finding a post outside Germany. However, it was not until David Cleghorn-Thomson, a representative of the Academic Assistance Council, visited the Emergency Committee in 1939 that complete clarification of the working relationship between the two organizations was obtained.

Dr. Walter Kotschnig, a distinguished young Austrian law scholar who spoke English admirably and had chosen to leave Germany because of his political and social views, arrived in the United States in the spring of 1936. He had served in 1935 as representative of our Committee and of the Notgemeinschaft deutscher Wissenschaftler im Ausland, in cooperating with the Academic Assistance Council in Europe. He had earlier acted as Director of the High Commission for Refugees Coming from Germany, of which James G. McDonald was Chairman. He was requested by the Emergency Committee to visit institutions in the Middle West to discover any additional needs that might be served by the Committee, and that could be learned only from personal discussion. Dr. Kotschnig, who had had wide experience with students and university administrators in Germany, was particularly well qualified for this investigation and performed an efficient job.

On a mission in Europe during 1934, the Secretary of the Emergency Committee, Dr. Duggan, was able to explore further the possibility of future relations with the overseas organizations working in the field. Two years later Dr. Alfred E. Cohn and Mr. Edward R. Murrow represented the Committee at meetings of the Experts' Committee and Advisory Council of the High Commission in London and studied measures to advance work in behalf of refugee scholars. The sum of $5,000 was appropriated at this time by the Emergency Committee to be expended in Europe for such purposes as would contribute most to the solution of the problem facing the deposed professors.

PRINCIPLES AND POLICIES OF THE EMERGENCY COMMITTEE

When the Emergency Committee was organized in May, 1933, the United States was in the midst of the Great Depression. Colleges and universities suffered with all other organizations and institutions. Enrollment of students dropped, and contributions to endowments were much diminished. With the difficulty of making both ends meet and with a lessened need for teachers, many of our institutions of higher education found it necessary to drop the younger and more recent additions to their staffs. Under such conditions, would not absorbing foreign teachers and research scholars cause resentment among our own university personnel? To meet this difficulty the Committee adopted certain policies which furthered its activities immensely.

Aware of the great number of scholars who would want to come to the United States to secure a position, larger by far than the number of positions available, the Committee decided to confine its efforts to displaced scholars of such eminence in their fields that there would be no thought of competition with young American scholars. The Committee decided also that it would not, save in exceptional cases, make grants for refugee scholars under thirty years of age or over sixty. In this respect its policy paralleled that of the Rockefeller Foundation and the Carnegie Corporation, both of which tended to reserve their funds for the support of distinguished older scholars who would not compete with younger Americans who had their way to make. In general, the Committee's help which was given in the form of grants-in-aid to colleges and universities in behalf of displaced scholars was limited to men and women who had been professors or at least Privatdozenten (or the equivalent) in European universities.

Of greater importance was the decision, adhered to for some years, to make no direct grant to an individual scholar. The request for a grant must come from a college or university, which would indicate the scholar it wanted and express willingness to disburse our stipend in his behalf in the form of salary payments. The Committee did, however, keep a list of displaced scholars seeking positions, so that if an institution should ask for the services of one in any field, a candidate could be provided. This procedure removed all possibility of misinterpreting the motives of the Committee as being actuated by charity in any ordinary sense of the term. It was of great importance that the personal pride of the refugee scholar, often the chief support of his morale, should not be undermined.

In passing, it might be mentioned that the number of displaced scholars and professional people in Europe who appealed to the Committee finally exceeded 6,000. The Committee could expect to place only a small part of them. Because of the eminence of the scholars who received invitations during the early career of the Committee and because of the fact that their salaries came not from the college budgets but from outside sources, American college teachers did not appear resentful to any marked degree.

In the early years of its history the Committee usually made a grant of $2,000 a year to an institution toward the salary of each displaced scholar. If the institution could not place the scholar upon its own budget at the end of the academic year, the Committee sometimes renewed the grant for a second year. Preference was always given, however, to requests from institutions that gave promise of absorbing the scholars into their faculties at an early time. As the years passed, the situation of scholars in Germany grew worse, and the number of refugee scholars reaching the United States increased. Under such conditions the grant-in-aid for a scholar had progressively to be diminished until at the end of its career the Emergency Committee was unable to make a grant beyond $1,000 for one year. The rest of the sum necessary for adequate support of a refugee scholar came either from   cooperating agencies or from the college budget, or from both.

The expanded program of the Emergency Committee required constantly increased financial support. The Rosenwald Family Association, whose grant is described at length on page 72, contributed generously. National Refugee Service made large donations to the Committee's program. It is noteworthy that, although the Committee's program was nonsectarian, its financial support came almost exclusively from prominent Jewish foundations. Two to which the Committee was immensely indebted, and without whose assistance it would have been wholly unable to realize its objective, were the New York Foundation and the Nathan Hofheimer Foundation. During the twelve years' existence of the Emergency Committee the New York Foundation contributed to its work a total of $339,851, and the Nathan Hofheimer Foundation a total of $67,000. When one considers the tremendous demands made upon our Jewish citizens for the succor of their cruelly persecuted co-religionists throughout Europe, this tribute to Jewish reverence for scholarship and learning cannot be too strongly stressed. Nor can the Committee allow this occasion to pass without recording the continuous courtesy with which Messrs. Stein and Flexner were received when presenting the needs of the Emergency Committee to the Directors of the two Foundations.

The Emergency Committee offered no relief services to the scholars who came into its office. Refugees in need of personal counsel and guidance were referred to the voluntary service agencies throughout the city according to the nature of their problem and in accordance with their religious preference. The Committee depended upon the testimony of colleagues in the academic world, and upon the evidence of such documents as its clients could bring with them out of Europe, to establish their standing in the world of scholarship. As to their personal problems, it listened sympathetically to such confidences as they might wish to unfold; but it sought always to respect the essential human dignity of the troubled persons who came to it. If a client found relief in speaking of absent wife and children, or in pouring out the pent-up misery induced by religious persecution followed by bitter and often grim experiences in the concentration camps, a quiet and receptive listener was present. At no time, however, was the refugee asked specific, point-blank questions about his intimate problems—except in so far as they touched upon the particular area in which the committee could render service—any more than he was asked to state his religious faith or racial background. The Committee tried by every means at its disposal to maintain an atmosphere in which the scholar would feel at ease and relaxed—accepted as an academician in an academic setting. The aim was through an understanding and sensible appraisal of his difficulties to help him use his own abilities to best advantage.

One fear that disturbed the Committee in the beginning of its career was not realized to any considerable extent; namely, the fear that anti-Semitism might be aroused in our colleges and universities because most of the displaced scholars seeking positions were Jews. Anti-Semitism was found in a few places, but they were very few. One flagrant case occurred in an eastern college where a scholar who had apparently given satisfaction from the standpoint of scholarship was dropped because of incompatibility with the head of the department. The professor who investigated the matter and reported his findings to the Emergency Committee wrote as follows:

I have known X for eight or ten years and have always considered him a thoroughly competent Germanist—keenly intelligent and scholarly, and a very attractive personality. I also know Professor Y, whose actions I can only explain as the instinctive emotional reactions of a native German to the blood and soil doctrine—a phenomenon I have observed often in some of our German-born colleagues.

I know there is a tendency among college teachers to assume that when a colleague is dismissed there must be reasons other than those generally stated—"The man must be difficult to get along with, etc." But I have lived so close to the emotional atmosphere of the present war years that I am convinced that, whatever truth there may be in such mental reservations at other times and places, X was dismissed for one reason only—his outspoken and determined criticism of Nazi Germany.

Such a case, however, was most unusual.

Our decision to limit our task to securing positions for refugee university scholars brought us some heartbreaks. One late afternoon after the staff had gone home a fine-looking man with tragedy written on his countenance entered Dr. Duggan's office unannounced. "What can I do for you, sir?" said Dr. Duggan. "I am one of the displaced Germans," answered the visitor. "Were you a university scholar?" inquired Dr. Duggan. "No, I was the statistician of the city of —————," answered the man. "I am sorry," said Dr. Duggan, "but this Committee confines its work to service to displaced scholars. However, there are some bankers on my Board of Trustees, and I shall be glad to give you letters of introduction to them." "I have already visited bankers," said the visitor, "and they cannot help me." "Then I shall give you letters to some industrialists whom I know," said Dr. Duggan. "I have talked with a number of industrialists but without any result," said the man. "Then I am sorry," said Dr. Duggan, "but I fear I do not know how to help you."

"I haven't a dollar left," answered the visitor. "What am I to do with my wife and children?"

He was not the kind of man whom one wanted to offer money to, or refer to a relief agency; yet his was inevitably a relief case. It did not require many experiences of that kind, and unfortunately there were many, to impress upon us the extent and degree of tragedy wrought by the atrocious conduct of the Nazi government.

The Emergency Committee was organized in the spirit of the Declaration of Independence. It served as a protest in defense of the dignity of man regardless of race, creed, or political opinion. It was guided by a determination that in the domain of the spirit intolerance and repression should have no place. It adhered to a decision that the teaching of youth should be based solely upon truth, without restriction upon teacher or student. It was particularly fitting that such an organization should be founded in the United States, whose very existence depends upon freedom, and whose Constitution provides for freedom of speech, of press, and of worship.

In carrying out these great principles, Americans have not differentiated between the citizen and the alien, the native and the immigrant. It was nevertheless very human that, among those who joined us from the old world in the desire to help build a better new world, the men and women whose vocation was concerned with the life of the spirit should receive a particular welcome. The mass of immigrants who came to our shores were persons who could help develop our country in a material sense and improve their own personal status while doing so. This was not true of the displaced scholar. It was almost inevitable that he should receive a lessened material reward and possibly fall to a lower social status than he had enjoyed in his native land. His great reward for flight here was the chance to continue work in the vocation for which he had made such prolonged preparation, and in which he had become adept. He hoped that he could do so in comparative freedom of mind.

The authors believe that the displaced scholars have kept the faith and have contributed largely to the spiritual life of our country; and they believe also that our country as symbolized by its institutions of learning has realized at least in part the spirit of its great Declaration in extending "life, liberty, and the pursuit of happiness" to this group of splendid scholars.

FIELDS OF SPECIALIZATION OF EMERGENCY COMMITTEE SCHOLARS, NATIONAL RESEARCH ASSOCIATES, AND ROSENWALD FELLOWS *

	Emergency Committee Scholars	National Research Associates	Rosenwald Fellows	Total
HUMANITIES	104	4	29	137
Archaeology	6	..	..	6
Architecture	1	..	..	1
Art, Applied	2	..	8	10
Art, History of	14	2	5	21
Education	5	..	1	6
Language and Literature	39	1	3	43
Letters	2	..	8	10
Music	7	..	1	8
Musicology	9	..	1	10
Philosophy	19	1	2	22
MEDICAL SCIENCES	7	..	..	7
Gynecology	1	..	..	1
Pathology	1	..	..	1
Physiology	2	..	..	2
Psychiatry	1	..	..	1
Public Health	1	..	..	1
Radiology	1	..	..	1
NATURAL SCIENCES	78	2	1	81
Astronomy	5	1	..	6
Biology	8	..	..	8
Chemistry	7	..	..	7
Engineering	2	..	..	2
Geography	1	..	..	1
Mathematics	26	..	..	26
Meteorology	1	1	..	2
Paleontology	2	..	..	2
Physics	16	..	..	16
Psychology	10	..	1	11
SOCIAL SCIENCES	88	5	17	110
Anthropology	2	..	..	2
Economics	26	2	5	33
History	16	..	3	19
Law	26	3	4	33
Political Science	8	..	1	9
Sociology	10	..	4	14

* In attempting to establish the field of specialization as of the time of the stipendiaries' arrival in the United States, the authors sought the direct cooperation of Scholars, Associates, and Fellows. In certain cases the field has been changed since the time of arrival. A number of Scholars in the field of law, for example, have turned to language teaching and political science since coming to this country.

APPENDIX II

DISTRIBUTION OF EMERGENCY COMMITTEE SCHOLARS, NATIONAL RESEARCH ASSOCIATES,* AND ROSENWALD FELLOWS,† ACCORDING TO AGE GROUPS

Age to Nearest Year	As of 1947 ‡				At Time of Initial Stipend			
	Scholars	National Research Associates	Rosenwald Fellows	Total	Scholars	National Research Associates	Rosenwald Fellows	Total
25–29	..	..	..	..	11	..	..	11
30–34	2	..	..	2	28	..	..	28
35–39	16	..	..	16	57	..	4	61
40–44	29	..	4	33	49	..	13	62
45–49	56	..	13	69	45	..	8	53
50–54	45	..	8	53	37	..	8	45
55–59	39	..	9	48	26	4	7	37
60–64	27	1	6	34	15	6	3	24
65–69	28	2	1	31	4	..	..	4
70–74	8	5	..	13	1	..	1	2
75–85	3	..	1	4	1	..	..	1
Unknown	3	..	3	6	3	1	3	7
Deceased	21	3	2	26	..	..	..	..
Total	277	11	47	335	277	11	47	335

From the above data it will be evident that the Emergency Committee concentrated its efforts on mature scholars and scientists. These men and women had already secured a firm place in the world of scholarship and in professional life, or held out a rich promise of future development. It was the Committee's belief that, on the part of this group, competition in the economic sense with American teachers and professional personnel could hardly be said to exist, since the contributions of these men and women were in most cases unique.

---

* The 11 National Research Associates include 2 men, previously Scholars, who appeared on the roll of Associates for one year only by special arrangement. They appear on all tables among the National Research Associates and not among the Committee's Scholars.

† The 47 Rosenwald Fellows include 5 men who also received Grants-in-Aid prior or subsequent to their term as Fellows, but who are nowhere tabulated as Scholars for statistical purposes.

‡ Ages of deceased not distributed.

APPENDIX III

COUNTRIES IN WHICH EMERGENCY COMMITTEE SCHOLARS, NATIONAL RESEARCH ASSOCIATES, AND ROSENWALD FELLOWS HAD BEEN ACTIVE PROFESSIONALLY

Country	Scholars	National Research Associates	Rosenwald Fellows	Total
Austria	31	4	14	49
Belgium	1	..	..	1
China	1 *	..	..	1
Czechoslovakia	8	..	1	9
France	5	..	3	8
Germany	207	7	25	239
Italy	9	..	1	10
Norway	1	..	..	1
Poland	4	..	1	5
Spain	4	..	..	4
Switzerland	1	..	..	1
Yugoslavia	1	..	..	1
Various	4	..	2	6
	277	11	47	335

For descriptive purposes, it was thought best to take into account the foreign country with which Scholars, National Research Associates, or Rosenwald Fellows had been most prominently or significantly associated during their professional life, rather than to tabulate countries either of birth or of last citizenship.

The place of birth does not necessarily indicate the locus in which the stipendiary's mature life has been passed, inasmuch as many of the men and women on the Committee's list spent their most active and productive years in countries other than those in which they were born. Of three artists on the Committee's list who were active in France, for example, one was born in Russia, one in Italy, and one in Austria.

Neither does country of last European citizenship furnish too valuable a

* A German national who spent many years in China.

clue to the geographic or cultural area within which the stipendiary's major contribution has been made, since in certain cases citizenship was acquired as a matter of expediency from a country of temporary asylum when the individual was driven from the nation in which his own scientific or professional development had taken place.

For these reasons, the country of major or longest professional activity seemed to have greater significance than other nationality factors in determining the origin of the Emergency Committee's stipendiaries.

APPENDIX IV

NUMBER AND AVERAGE SIZE OF GRANTS-IN-AID ACCORDING TO ACADEMIC YEARS

Academic Year	Number of Grants-in-Aid	Amount of Average Grant-in-Aid
1933–34	30	$1,856.67 *
1934–35	51	1,716.11
1935–36	47	1,696.81
1936–37	33	1,592.55
1937–38	46	1,456.79
1938–39	49	1,345.45
1939–40	68	1,008.09
1940–41	109	898.87
1941–42	78 †	802.43 †
1942–43	69 †	831.40 †
1943–44	36 †	898.61 †
1944–45	14 †	646.43 †

The Emergency Committee's National Research Associates plan commenced during the academic year 1941–42 and has continued since that time. The Rosenwald Fellowships project started the following academic year and was concluded before the end of the academic year 1944–45.

As both of these were separate projects financed from special funds which made possible the maintenance of a uniformly higher scale of stipend than could be given under the Committee's Grant-in-Aid program, it did not seem proper to take them into consideration when figuring the average yearly grant available for Emergency Committee stipendiaries. The above table includes, therefore, only Grants-in-Aid given under the Committee's regular program.

---

* Figure adjusted to reflect rate for a full academic year. Many scholars during the Committee's first twelve months did not reach the United States until the academic year was well advanced. Compensation received by them out of funds supplied by the Committee was accordingly prorated. To present as a figure for the academic year the average of sums actually received for portions of the year varying in length from one scholar to another would, therefore, give a false picture. Instead, an estimate has been given of what the average stipend would have been for the full academic year.

† Exclusive of National Research Associates' stipends or Rosenwald Fellowships.

APPENDIX V

NUMBER OF YEARS THE EMERGENCY COMMITTEE HAS ASSISTED
EACH OF ITS 335 SCHOLARS, NATIONAL RESEARCH ASSO-
CIATES, AND ROSENWALD FELLOWS, AS AT THE
CLOSE OF ITS WORK IN 1945

156 persons were assisted for no more than one year.
82 persons were assisted for no more than two years.
46 persons were assisted for no more than three years.
19 persons were assisted for no more than four years.
16 persons were assisted for no more than five years.
13 persons were assisted for no more than six years.
2 persons were assisted for no more than seven years.
1 person was assisted for ten years.

APPENDIX VI

INSTITUTIONS WHICH RECEIVED GRANTS FROM THE
EMERGENCY COMMITTEE

Albright Art Gallery, Buffalo
American Academy for Jewish Research, New York
American Law Institute, Philadelphia
American Museum of Natural History, New York
American University, Washington, D.C.
Antioch College, Yellow Springs, Ohio
Atlanta University, Atlanta
Barat College of the Sacred Heart, Lake Forest, Ill.
Barnard College, Columbia University, New York
Bennett College, Greensboro, N.C.
Black Mountain College, Black Mountain, N.C.
Boston University, Boston
Brookings Institution, Washington, D.C.
Brooklyn College, Brooklyn, N.Y.
Brown University, Providence, R.I.
Bryn Mawr College, Bryn Mawr, Pa.
University of Buffalo, Buffalo
University of California, Berkeley
Carnegie Institute of Technology, Pittsburgh
Catholic University of America, Washington, D.C.
Central Y.M.C.A. College (now Roosevelt College), Chicago
University of Chicago, Chicago
Claremont Colleges, Claremont, Calif.
Coe College, Cedar Rapids, Iowa
Colby College, Waterville, Maine
Columbia University, New York

Connecticut College, New London
Converse College, Spartanburg, S.C.
Cornell University, Ithaca, N.Y.
University of Denver, Denver, Colo.
Dubuque University, Dubuque, Iowa
Duke University, Durham, N.C.
Duquesne University, Pittsburgh
East Indies Institute of America, New York
Elmhurst College, Elmhurst, Ill.
Erskine College, Due West, S.C.
Fenn College, Cleveland
Field Museum of Natural History, Chicago
Fletcher School of Law and Diplomacy, Medford, Mass.
Fordham University, New York
University of Georgia, Athens, Ga.
Guilford College, Guilford College, N.C.
Hamilton College, Clinton, N.Y.
Harvard University, Cambridge, Mass.
Hebrew University, Jerusalem
Hobart College, Geneva, N.Y.
Howard University, Washington, D.C.
Illinois College, Jacksonville
Illinois Institute of Technology, Chicago
Indiana University, Bloomington, Ind.
Institute for Advanced Study, Princeton, N.J.
Institute of Pacific Relations, New York
Institute of Social Research, New York
Iowa State College of Agriculture and Mechanic Arts, Ames
State University of Iowa, Iowa City
Iranian Institute and School for Asiatic Studies, New York
Jewish Institute of Religion, New York
College of Jewish Studies, Chicago
Jewish Theological Seminary of America, New York
Johns Hopkins University, Baltimore
University of Kansas, Lawrence
University of Kansas City, Kansas City, Mo.
Kent State University, Kent, Ohio
University of Kentucky, Lexington
Kenyon College, Gambier, Ohio
Lawrence College, Appleton, Wis.
Library of Congress, Washington, D.C.
Longy School of Music, Cambridge, Mass.
University of Louisville, Louisville, Ky.
Marquette University, Milwaukee, Wis.
Mary Washington College, Fredericksburg, Va.
Massachusetts Institute of Technology, Cambridge
Miami University, Oxford, Ohio
University of Michigan, Ann Arbor
Mills College, Mills College, Calif.

Milton College, Milton, Wis.
University of Minnesota, Minneapolis
Mount Holyoke College, South Hadley, Mass.
Mount Union College, Alliance, Ohio
Museum of Fine Arts, Boston
University of New Hampshire, Durham
New Jersey College for Women, New Brunswick
University of New Mexico, Albuquerque
New School for Social Research, New York
College of the City of New York, New York
New York Public Library, New York
New York State Psychiatric Institute and Hospital, New York
New York University, New York
H. Sophie Newcomb Memorial College for Women, Tulane University, New Orleans
University of North Carolina, Chapel Hill
Northwestern University, Evanston, Ill.
Ohio State University, Columbus
Olivet College, Olivet, Mich.
Our Lady of the Lake College, San Antonio, Texas
Pacific School of Religion, Berkeley, Calif.
Parsons College, Fairfield, Iowa
Pendle Hill, Wallingford, Pa.
Pennsylvania State College, State College
University of Pennsylvania, Philadelphia
Pomona College, Claremont, Calif.
Princeton University, Princeton, N.J.
Purdue University, Lafayette, Ind.
Queens College of the City of New York, Flushing, N.Y.
Rand School of Social Science, New York
Richmond Professional Institute of the College of William and Mary, Richmond, Va.
Rockford College, Rockford, Ill.
Rockland State Hospital, Orangeburg, N.Y.
Rutgers University, New Brunswick, N.J.
St. John's College, Annapolis, Md.
St. John's University, Brooklyn, N.Y.
St. Lawrence University, Canton, N.Y.
St. Michael's College, Winooski Park, Vt.
College of St. Thomas, St. Paul, Minn.
University of Scranton, Scranton, Pa.
Settlement Music School, Philadelphia
Smith College, Northampton, Mass.
University of the South, Sewanee, Tenn.
University of Southern California, Los Angeles
Southern Illinois Normal University, Carbondale
Southwestern, Memphis, Tenn.
Stanford University, Stanford University, Calif.
Swarthmore College, Swarthmore, Pa.

Teachers College, Columbia University, New York
Temple University, Philadelphia
University of Toledo, Toledo, Ohio
Union Theological Seminary, New York
U.S. Government, Bureau of the Census, Washington, D.C.
Vanderbilt University, Nashville, Tenn.
Vassar College, Poughkeepsie, N.Y.
University of Virginia, Charlottesville
Washington University, St. Louis
Wayne County Training School, Northville, Mich.
Wayne University, Detroit
Wellesley College, Wellesley, Mass.
Wesleyan University, Middletown, Conn.
West Virginia State College, Institute
Western Reserve University, Cleveland
Westminster Choir College, Princeton, N.J.
Wilson College, Chambersburg, Pa.
Winthrop College, Rock Hill, S.C.
University of Wisconsin, Madison
Worcester Polytechnic Institute, Worcester, Mass.
Yale University, New Haven, Conn.
Yankton College, Yankton, S.D.
Yiddish Scientific Institute, New York

APPENDIX VII

GEOGRAPHICAL DISTRIBUTION OF EMERGENCY COMMITTEE SCHOLARS, ROSENWALD FELLOWS, AND NATIONAL RESEARCH ASSOCIATES *

CALIFORNIA 16
    University of California, Berkeley   8
    Claremont Colleges   1
    Mills College   1
    Pacific School of Religion   1
    Pomona College   1
    University of Southern California   1
    Stanford University   3
COLORADO 1
    University of Denver   1
CONNECTICUT 11
    Connecticut College   1
    Wesleyan University   1
    Yale University   9

* A number of individuals have been assisted at more than one institution, and their presence at each institution has been indicated and counted separately.

DISTRICT OF COLUMBIA 19
    American University 5
    Brookings Institution 3
    The Catholic University 3
    Howard University 2
    Library of Congress 5
    United States Government, Bureau of Census 1

GEORGIA 3
    Atlanta University 1
    University of Georgia 2

ILLINOIS 26
    Barat College of the Sacred Heart 1
    Central Y.M.C.A. College (now Roosevelt College) 5
    University of Chicago 9
    Elmhurst College 1
    Field Museum of Natural History 1
    Illinois College 1
    Illinois Institute of Technology 1
    College of Jewish Studies 1
    Northwestern University 3
    Rockford College 2
    Southern Illinois Normal University 1

INDIANA 2
    Indiana University 1
    Purdue University 1

IOWA 5
    Coe College 1
    University of Dubuque 1
    Iowa State College of Agriculture and Mechanic Arts 1
    Parsons College 1
    State University of Iowa 1

KANSAS 1
    University of Kansas 1

KENTUCKY 6
    University of Kentucky 2
    University of Louisville 4

LOUISIANA 1
    H. Sophie Newcomb Memorial College 1

MAINE 1
    Colby College 1

MARYLAND 10
    Johns Hopkins University 9
    St. John's College 1

MASSACHUSETTS 27
    Boston University 1
    Fletcher School of Law and Diplomacy 2

Harvard University	13
Longy School of Music	1
Massachusetts Institute of Technology	4
Mount Holyoke College	2
Museum of Fine Arts, Boston	1
Smith College	1
Wellesley College	1
Worcester Polytechnic Institute	1

MICHIGAN 5
University of Michigan	2
Olivet College	1
Wayne County Training School	1
Wayne University	1

MINNESOTA 2
University of Minnesota	1
College of St. Thomas	1

MISSOURI 5
University of Kansas City	2
Washington University	3

NEW HAMPSHIRE 1
University of New Hampshire	1

NEW JERSEY 18
Institute for Advanced Study	11
New Jersey College for Women	1
Princeton University	2
Rutgers University	3
Westminster Choir College	1

NEW MEXICO 1
University of New Mexico	1

NEW YORK 111
Albright Art Gallery	1
American Academy for Jewish Research	4
American Museum of Natural History	2
Barnard College	1
Brooklyn College	2
University of Buffalo	1
College of the City of New York	3
Columbia University	13
Cornell University	3
East Indies Institute of America	1
Fordham University	2
Hamilton College	1
Hobart College	1
Institute of Pacific Relations	1
Institute of Social Research	11
Iranian Institute and School for Asiatic Studies	7
Jewish Institute of Religion	1

Jewish Theological Seminary	2
New School for Social Research	21
New York Public Library	6
New York State Psychiatric Institute and Hospital	1
New York University	13
Queens College	1
Rand School of Social Science	1
Rockland State Hospital	1
St. John's University	1
St. Lawrence University	1
Teachers College	1
Union Theological Seminary	1
Vassar College	5
Yiddish Scientific Institute	1

NORTH CAROLINA	**7**
Bennett College	1
Black Mountain College	1
Duke University	2
Guilford College	1
University of North Carolina	2

OHIO	**9**
Antioch College	1
Fenn College	1
Kent State University	1
Kenyon College	1
Miami University	1
Mount Union College	1
Ohio State University	1
University of Toledo	1
Western Reserve University	1

PENNSYLVANIA	**27**
American Law Institute	1
Bryn Mawr College	5
Carnegie Institute of Technology	1
Duquesne University	1
Pendle Hill	1
Pennsylvania State College	1
University of Pennsylvania	8
University of Scranton	1
Settlement Music School, Philadelphia	1
Swarthmore College	5
Temple University	1
Wilson College	1

RHODE ISLAND	**2**
Brown University	2

SOUTH CAROLINA	**3**
Converse College	1
Erskine College	1
Winthrop College	1

APPENDIX VIII

A. THE 288 DISPLACED SCHOLARS (INCLUDING NATIONAL RESEARCH ASSOCIATES) ASSISTED THROUGH THE EMERGENCY COMMITTEE, AND THEIR FIELDS OF STUDY *

Hanokh Albeck, Talmudic Studies
Berthold Altmann, History
Eugen Altschul, Economics
Valentin Bargmann, Physics
David Baumgardt, Philosophy
Guido Beck (a), Physics
Maximilian Beck, Philosophy
Walter Beck (a), Psychology
Richard Behrendt, International Affairs
Adolf Berger, Law

Gustav Bergmann, Mathematics
Ernst Berl, Chemistry
Felix Bernstein, Mathematics
Hans Beutler (b), Physics
Margarete Bieber, Archaeology
Erwin Reinhold Biel, Meteorology
Justus Bier, History of Art
Felix Bloch, Physics
Erwin Bodky, Music
Werner A. Bohnstedt, Sociology
Enzo Joseph Bonaventura, Psychology

* In these lists a parenthetic *a* signifies, Returned to Europe; *b*, Deceased; *c*, Nobel Prize winner; *d*, Served in U.S. Army; *e*, Served at Biarritz (France) American University, 1946; *f*, Formerly a grantee of the Committee; *g*, Subsequently a grantee of the Committee.

Curt Bondy, Education
Theodor von Brand, Biology
Alfred T. Brauer, Mathematics
Richard Brauer, Mathematics
Theodor Brauer (b), Economics
Kurt Braun, Economics
Otto Brendel, Archaeology
Warner F. Brook (b), Economics
Eberhard Friedrich Bruck, Law
Martin Buber, Philosophy
Manfred Bukofzer, Musicology
Walter V. Burg, Chemistry
Hans Cassel, Chemistry
Umberto Moshe David Cassuto, Philology
Gustave Cohen (a), Literature
Sigmund Cohn, Law
Ernst Cohn-Wiener (b), History of Art
Victor Conrad, Meteorology
Richard Courant, Mathematics
Heinz Dallmann, Law
Max Dehn, Mathematics
Max Delbrück, Physics
Leonid Doljanski, Pathology
Adolph B. Drucker, Economics
Ludwig Edelstein, Philology
Tilly Edinger, Paleontology
Maximilian Ehrenstein, Chemistry
Friedrich Engel-Janosi, History
Fritz Epstein, History
Richard Ettinghausen, History of Art
Ladislaus Farkas, Chemistry
Bruno Fels, Statistics
William Fiedler, Music
Eva Fiesel (b), Linguistics
Ossip K. Flechtheim, Political Science
Max Förster (a), Philology
Abraham Adolf Fraenkel, Mathematics
Hermann Fraenkel, Classics
James Franck (c), Physics
Louis R. Franck, Economics
Erich Frank, Philosophy
Philipp Frank, Physics
Oskar Frankl, Education
Paul Frankl, History of Art
Erich Franzen, Letters
Aron Freimann, Bibliography

Rudolf Freund, Economics
Hans Fried, Law
Hans Fried (b), Mathematics
Paul Friedlaender, Classical Philology
Walter Friedlaender, History of Art
Kurt Friedrichs, Mathematics
Walter Fuchs, Chemistry
William R. Gaede, Education
Felix M. Gatz (b), Musicology
Bernhard Geiger, Oriental Philology
Moritz Geiger (b), Philosophy
Hilda Geiringer, Mathematics
Karl Geiringer, Musicology
Melitta Gerhard, Literature
Felix Gilbert, History
Rudolf Glanz, Law
Kurt Gödel, Mathematics
Franz Goldmann, Public Health
G. E. von Grünebaum, Oriental Philology
Gotthard Günther, Philosophy
Wolfgang Guenther, Law
Emil J. Gumbel, Statistics
Herman S. Gundersheimer, History of Art
Julius Guttmann, Philosophy
Fritz Haas, Zoology
Otto H. Haas, Paleontology
William S. Haas, Sociology and Anthropology
Jacques Hadamard (a), Mathematics
Ludwig Halberstaedter, Radiology
Wolfgang Hallgarten (d), History
Ludwig Hamburger, Economics
Viktor Hamburger, Zoology
Joseph Hanč, Government Service
Willy Hartner (a), Astronomy
Werner Hegemann (b), Architecture and City Planning
Robert von Heine-Geldern, Ethnology
Ernst Hellinger, Mathematics
John L. Herma (d), Psychology
Léon Herrmann (a), Classical Literature
Gerhard Herz, Musicology
John H. Herz, Law
Ernst Emil Herzfeld, Archaeology
Artur von Hippel, Physics
Rudolf Höber, Physiology

Heinrich Hoeniger, Law
Oscar Hoffman, Engineering
Hajo Holborn, History
Richard Martin Honig, History and Philosophy of Law
Erich Hula, Law
Hugo Iltis, Biology
Luigi Jacchia, Astronomy
Ernest Jackh, International Relations
Fritz Jahoda, Music
Roman Jakobson, Philology
Fritz John, Mathematics
Victor Jollos (b), Zoology
Oswald Jonas, Musicology
Henry R. Kahane, Linguistics
Alfred Kähler, Economics
Richard A. Kahn, Economics and Public Administration
Franz Kallmann, Psychiatry
Ernst Kanitz, Music
Ernst Kantorowicz, History
Ernst Kapp, Classical Philology
Fritz Karsen, Education
Adolf Katzenellenbogen, History of Art
Felix Kaufmann, Philosophy
Fritz Kaufmann, Philosophy
Stephen S. Kayser, History of Art
Robert M. W. Kempner, Police Administration
Friedrich Kessler, Law
Hans Kirchberger, Law
Otto Kirchheimer, Law
Guido Kisch, Law
Jacob Klatzkin, Philosophy
Jacob Klein, History of Mathematics and Mathematical Physics
Richard Koebner, History
Zdenek Kopal, Astronomy
Siegfried Kraus, Sociology
Richard Krautheimer, History of Art
Manfred Kridl, Literature
Heinrich Kronstein, Law
Helmut Kuhn, Philosophy
Gustav Land, Astronomy
Carl Landauer, Economics
Oscar Lassner, Music
Rudolf von Laun (a), Law
Albert Lauterbach, Economics

Max Lederer, Language and Literature
Fritz Lehmann (b), Economics
Karl Lehmann (Lehmann-Hartleben), Archaeology
Frederick Lehner, Language and Literature
Arthur Lenhoff, Law
Friedrich Lenz, Classical Language and Literature
Wolf Leslau, Languages
Kurt Lewin (b), Psychology
Hans Lewy, Mathematics
Julius Lewy, Philology
Wolfgang Liepe, Language and Literature
Julius Lips, Anthropology
Karl Loewenstein, Law
Karl Loewner, Mathematics
Moritz Löwi (b), Psychology
Edward Lowinsky, Musicology
Erna Magnus, Sociology
Nicolai Malko, Music
Alfred Manes, Insurance and Economics
Ernst Manheim, Sociology
Fritz Karl Mann, Economics
Thomas Mann (c), Letters
Siegfried Marck, Philosophy
Herbert Marcuse, Philosophy
Jacques Maritain (a), Philosophy
Carl Mayer, Sociology
Karl W. Meissner, Physics
Kaethe Mengelberg, Economics
Julie Meyer, Sociology
Kathi Meyer-Baer, Musicology
Franz Michael, Chinese History and Far Eastern Affairs
Rudolf Minkowski, Physics
Hans Morgenthau, Law
Otto Nathan, Economics
Alfons Nehring, Philology
Hans Neisser, Economics
Paul Nettl, Musicology
Otto Neugebauer, Mathematics
Franz Neumann, Economics
Sigmund Neumann, Sociology
Robert Neuner, Law
Emmy Noether (b), Mathematics

Lothar Wolfgang Nordheim, Physics
Arthur Nussbaum, Law
Leonardo Olschki, Philology
Oskar Oppenheimer, Psychology
Melchior Palyi, Economics
Wolfgang Paulsen, Language and Literature
Alexander H. Pekelis (b), Law
Nicolás Percas, Languages
Georg Petschek (b), Law
Kurt Pinthus, History of Literature and of the Theater
Willibald Ploechl, Law
Ernst Posner, Archives Administration
Richard Prager (b), Astronomy
Karl Pribram, Economics
Peter Pringsheim, Physics
Luis Quintanilla, Painting
Ernst Rabel, Law
Giulio Racah, Physics
Hans Rademacher, Mathematics
Hermann Ranke (a), Archaeology
Egon Ranshofen-Wertheimer, Political Science
Franz J. Rapp, History of Theater Art
Anton Raubitschek, Archaeology
Victor Regener, Physics
Fritz Reiche, Physics
Max Rheinstein, Law
Werner Richter, Language and Literature
Fernando de los Ríos, Political Science
Arthur Rosenberg (b), History
Hans Rosenberg, History
Hans Rosenberg (a, b), Astronomy
Arthur Rosenthal, Mathematics
Herbert Rosinski, Military and Naval Theory
Bruno Rossi, Physics
Curt Sachs, Musicology
Alfred Salmony, History of Art
Richard Salomon, History
Arthur Salz, Economics
Martin Scheerer, Psychology
Guido Schoenberger, History of Art
Alfred Schuhmann, Philosophy

Heinrich Schwarz, History of Art
Rudolf Schwenger, Economics
Anna Selig, Education
Friedrich Sell, Language and Literature
Carl L. Siegel, Mathematics
Rolf Singer, Mycology
Sigmund Skard (a), Literature
Karl Sollner, Chemistry
Friedrich Solmsen, Classics
Clemens Sommer, History of Art
Martin Sommerfeld (b), Language and Literature
Alexander Sperber, Philology
Friedrich Spiegelberg, Philosophy
Herbert Spiegelberg, Philosophy
Diether von den Steinen, Languages
Hugo Steiner-Prag (b), Graphic Arts
William Stern (b), Psychology
Richard Stoehr, Music
Walter Sulzbach, Economics
Otto Szasz, Mathematics
Gabor Szegö (e), Mathematics
Alfred Tarski, Mathematics and Logic
Paul Tedesco, Philology
Paul Tillich, Philosophy
Dinko Tomasic, Sociology
Harry Torczyner, Philology
Otto Treitel, Botany
Curt Victorius, Economics
Werner F. Vogel, Engineering
Leo Waibel, Geography
Gotthold Weil, Philology
Martin Weinbaum, History
Martin Weinberger, History of Art
Sucher B. Weinryb, Talmudic Studies
Herbert Weinschel, Political Science
Richard Weissenberg, Zoology
Heinz Werner, Psychology
Ernst Wertheimer, Physiology
Helene Wieruszowski, History
Ernst Karl Winter, Government Service
Rachel Wischnitzer-Bernstein, History of Art
Karl A. Wittfogel, History of Chinese Institutions and Society
Hans Julius Wolff, Law

Werner Wolff, Psychology
Leo Wollemborg, History
Sergius Yakobson, Philology
Edgar Zilsel *(b)*, Philosophy

Heinrich Zimmer *(b)*, Philosophy
Bernard Zondek, Gynecology
Antoni Zygmund, Mathematics

B. THE 47 ROSENWALD FELLOWS OF THE EMERGENCY COMMITTEE AND THEIR FIELDS OF SPECIALIZATION AT TIME OF ARRIVAL IN UNITED STATES

Marc Abramowitsch, Sociology
Hans Baron, History
Klaus Berger *(e)*, History of Art
Josef Berolzheimer, Economics
Beate Berwin, Language and Literature
Egon Vitalis Biel, Painting
Ferdinand Bruckner, Play Writing
Renata Calabresi, Psychology
Adolf Caspary, Political Science
Ladislas Czettel *(f)*, Costume Design
Albert Ehrenstein, Letters
Susanne Engelmann, Education
Walter Fales, Philosophy
Ilse Falk, History of Art
Julius Fischer *(b)*, Law
Ruth Fischer, Sociology
Joseph Floch, Painting
Bernhard Ganzel, Geography
Judith Grunfeld, Economics
Eugen Guerster-Steinhausen, Letters
Ivan Heilbut, Letters
Hans Heymann *(f)*, Economics
Emil Kaufmann, History of Art
Simon Lissim, Decorative Arts

Raphael Mahler, History
Hugo Marx, Law
Paul W. Massing, Economics
Artur Michel, History of the Dance
Kurt Nadelmann, Law
Toni Oelsner, Sociology
Adolf Leo Oppenheim *(f)*, Oriental Philology
Karl Otto Paetel, Letters
Robert Pick, Letters
Victor Polzer, Letters
Rudolf Ray, Painting
Bernard Reder, Sculpture
Hans Sahl, Letters
Berta Segall *(f)*, History of Art
Alfred Sendrey, Musicology
George Stefansky, Philosophy
Victor Tischler, Painting
Ludwig Ullmann, History of the Theatre
Veit Valentin *(b, f)*, History
Dario Viterbo, Sculpture
Hedwig Wachenheim, Social Work
Karl Weigl *(g)*, Music
Frederick Welt, Law

Index

209

Date Due

FEB 14 '49			